Susan Wicks grew up in Kent and stud... ... of Hull and Sussex, where she wrote ... André Gide. She has taught in Franc... Dublin. She now lives with her husband and two daughters in Tunbridge Wells, and works as a part-time tutor for the University of Kent.

SUSAN WICKS

ff

faber and faber

LONDON · BOSTON

First published in 1995
by Faber and Faber Limited
3 Queen Square London WC1N 3AU
This paperback edition first published in 1997

Photoset by Wilmaset Ltd, Wirral
Printed and bound in Great Britain by
Mackays of Chatham PLC, Chatham, Kent

© Susan Wicks, 1995

Susan Wicks is hereby identified as author of this work
in accordance with Section 77 of the Copyright,
Designs and Patents Act 1988

A CIP record for this book
is available from the British Library

ISBN 0–571–17925–8

I would like to thank the Virginia Centre for the Creative Arts for
giving me the space and freedom to allow this book to come
into existence, and South-East Arts for making
the visit to Virginia possible. S.W.

2 4 6 8 10 9 7 5 3 1

for Emily and Bridget

Part One

I AM SITTING OUTSIDE in the sun, in sun-hat and sun-glasses, at the white plastic table. I've just had lunch. I'm rereading *L'Éducation sentimentale* for a French class I give every Wednesday evening. I hear the phone ring.

I go inside and answer it. As I pick up the receiver, my sun-glasses adjust to the light and the bookcase swims up out of the shadows, piled with papers and directories. The carpet is splashed with red from the stained glass in the front door.

It is my mother's friend, Julia. 'Susan?' Why would she ring me? I know at once that something is very wrong. 'Your father would like to speak to you.'

I wait. I hear a clunk as the receiver is passed from hand to hand. 'Daddy?'

And then a strange sound, an odd kind of high wailing. It isn't like anything I have ever heard, or could ever have imagined. It seems to grow to fill the corners of my house, getting higher and higher. I begin to make out words in it. 'She's gone, Joy's gone.' Then, 'She's dead.'

I think I manage to ask, 'When? How?'

And somehow he must manage to tell me.

When John and I get to my parents' house, my mother's body has already been taken away. Julia and Anne are still there, waiting for us to come. The first thing we see as we drive up to the front door is the bunch of pinks they brought, in a vase on the front window-sill. It is my mother's last gift.

My father is sitting at the dining-room table. The long curtains are almost drawn, as they always are in the summer. Through a vertical crack I can see a stripe of back fence in bright sunlight, covered with honeysuckle, a blazing tangle of pink and cream trumpets. The fat bees seem to hang in the air between them.

*

3

Every summer we would go to the seaside, to the caravan. My cousin and I would spend several weeks there, half of it with his parents and half with mine. That was when my father would fly the kites.

He would wait until there were one or two little diamond-kites or box-kites bobbing at the caravan window. Then he would look round at us. 'Well, then? Do you want to help me launch it? Come on, then. Be quick.'

It was always a matter of 'launching'. Ours weren't the kind of kites you had to run about with, looking foolish. Our kites didn't waste energy on appearances. They always looked awkward and heavy, like some brown-paper albatross. There was always a solid notched cane skeleton, an armful of tail and a bale of string wound on a lump of old wood.

By the time I was eleven I knew the technique well enough to do it on my own. But really it took two: one person to grasp the kite at the centre and raise it to the wind, and another to stand about thirty yards away, just beyond the tip of the tail, holding the string. I would try to read my father's mind. I would watch a strong gust coming towards me over the grass and I would look at him. And then he would shout, 'Now!'

And the great kite would rise straight up into the sky, the string unwinding, bouncing on the grass, hanging towards us in a great arc, the tail whipping our faces and then gone. And in the distance the square brown face would wobble against other currents, no bigger than a stamp. Within minutes we would find ourselves at the centre of a crowd of kids, all pointing and screaming out questions and wanting to take the string from my father's hands.

When my mother dies, the wooden sill of the patio doors is crammed with runner-bean seedlings. My father eventually manages to plant them in the garden, only a few weeks late. By the end of July we have more beans than we know what to do with. My Uncle Harry picks them and puts them in the fridge for me to find. My mother's sister, Mona, helps me to slice them and

4

blanch them for the freezer. In the end we lose patience and freeze them raw.

I can't manage to cut them as my mother did, to strip off the outer fibres neatly with a little bone-handled knife and then slice the flesh that is left into neat, equal slivers. I buy a sophisticated bean-slicer that will perform both operations simultaneously. Once I trap my own finger briefly in the top of it, and shudder, thinking how it could strip ribbons of skin from the two sides of my finger, and fan the rest into red pulp. But it is only a little nick. I suck the small wound, and it fills up again immediately with blood.

My mother was always slicing beans. That is how I remember our summers. Sitting on a child's wooden chair in the back garden, or on the caravan step with an enamel bowl in her lap, she would slice perfectly with her little knife, the paper-thin blade stained almost black, the chipped bone handle streaking. To me the waste from the beans looked like little green pointed hats with long straight green hair hanging from them. I can remember gathering up whole handfuls and playing with them, combing the green hair out with my hands. And it seems to me she was happy, sitting on that step in the sun with her bare legs shining, and the bowl balanced between them.

And where were the men? What were they doing as she sliced beans for our dinner? They would sit in the deckchairs. In the spring they repainted the 'doings'. In the night they would empty it in a hole, while we children were asleep.

And this is the smell of spring turning to summer – Elsan and Calor gas, runner-bean sap, seaweed strung up to dry, flapping at the door. And the sound and feel and taste of it: cuckoos in the woods, ladies' smocks waist-deep in the grass, the brown heads of sorrel. The eyes of anemones in the wood, shamrock at the edge of the path, the rusty oil-drums in the clearing, where the boys would beat out their war-cry. And the inside itself of the caravan, that heady mixture of paint and warm hardboard. The

5

round holes for your fingers. The knot-hole in the wall of the outhouse, where you could 'sit on' and look out, from the gloom inside to a twig that waved in and out of the sun.

My mother's underwear still lies across the back of a chair in the bedroom, where they left it the day she died. The wrinkled elastic of her bra is going grey at the edges. The big cups gape open.

My friends always loved my parents. 'Your mum's so kind,' they would tell me after they had stayed for the weekend. 'And your dad's really sweet.' My French penfriend, Arlette, once said to me, 'Your parents are two angels.'

Every week, when I go in, I find him sitting at the table, or standing in the kitchen with a dishcloth in his hand. He is always crying. Often I hear the strange unearthly sound of his keening as I turn my key in the lock.

Every week I take the shrivelled apples, the brown-tipped grapes dissolving in their own sweet juice, and dispose of them. Every week I wipe out the fruit-bowl and replace the wrinkled fruit with something fresh.

Sometimes, when I was younger, when my mother was alive, he would show us that we had hurt his feelings. He would vacate his usual armchair in its prime place next to the hearth, directly in front of the television, and relegate himself to her low chair on the edge of the circle. He would sit there not speaking until we made a fuss of him, until we protested that we loved him, and begged him to return. If we didn't, he would stay there in silence all evening.

My mother would usually crack first. I can still remember her voice, torn between affection and exasperation. 'Oh, Eric, *darling*. Do come and sit in your chair!' And he would come back, like a child. And she would try to make him feel better.

*

More and more now I begin to remember just what my mother *did* do for my father – not just the sugar in the stirred tea, but the washed hair, cut toenails, the eye-drops, the hand-knitted bed-socks in strange colours, the peeled tomatoes and peaches, the filled hot-water bottles, the cooked green vegetables softened with bicarbonate of soda.

Every old man I see now is a part of my father. This one, shambling to the post-box in crumpled grey and camel. Or this one, blinking at me through his shrunken field of vision, and smiling too late in greeting. This one fumbling with his pension book in the sub-post office. This one who can't reach to open his car door, caught in the webbing belt locked at his shoulder. Or this one shuffling his bare blue feet in sandals, his crazy monologue filling the shop doorways. Or my father himself, crying into greasy water.

I sit in the car waiting for Bridget to come out of her dancing lesson, and I think that dying must be like this. Sitting still and sleepy as the light is fading, seeing raindrops on the glass like mercury, seeing them slowly gather and then run suddenly down into darkness, leaving a transparent path where you can see flowers, the walls of houses, other windows. Not thinking 'tears', but only 'transparent'. For there to be no speed but this, no position but this, no life but this waiting. The sun-roof with its surface of tiny dots is like newsprint. The trees are like trees in a newspaper, their limbs reducible to a rational pattern of dots.

My mother hated driving. She would avoid it if she could. But occasionally she would find herself in a situation where she was forced to get into the driver's seat.

Every few months she would have to drive me to Oxted, to the dentist, the two of us in the old Morris, frozen in our separate anxieties. I can remember her trying to back the car out of the dentist's drive and being hooted at by another motorist. I can still see her taking her hands from the wheel to cover her face.

*

7

My father's shyness was legendary. He would tell me how much more confidence and freedom there was in my adolescence than there had been in his own. 'I wouldn't have *spoken* to a girl, until I was seventeen!' he would say.

And he would put his arm round my mother and pull her closer to him. And she would laugh.

My father was shy. Sometimes when we had visitors, my mother would have to smooth things over. He would be quiet in a corner, or retreat upstairs.

But sometimes he would suddenly take the stage, talking and talking. His whole face would light up.

'You monopolized them!' my mother would accuse him afterwards. 'They're *my* friends! And you never let me get a word in edgeways!'

My father looks at me, his face wet with tears. 'It was so *cruel* that she was taken from me!'

Cruel of whom? I ask myself. Cruelty implies belief. But my father doesn't believe in a God, only in His sadism. He is a victim. He was always a victim. But there is no aggressor. His need. He has no interest in anything but that.

My parents hardly ever quarrelled. When they did, I could never tell whether they were serious. Sometimes, in sheer exasperation, my mother would throw the wet dishcloth at my father's head. And he would pick it up and throw it back.

And then it would become a kind of game, my mother hurling the grey cotton cloth as hard as she could and screaming at him, and my father aiming it back at her. And I would scream too. And before long I had joined in, the three of us jumping to catch the cloth as it flew across the kitchen, pelting one another indiscriminately, hysterical with laughter.

Every Thursday I go over to have lunch with him. Shortly after eleven I load the car with his groceries and clean laundry and set out, the casserole of lunch clanking in the back as I turn corners. On the passenger seat beside me I have his little black tape-recorder. On the switchback road dappled with sun I listen to Mozart or Sibelius. I drive through whirling leaves, a swarm of bees, a flock of ragged crows.

These are the best moments of my life, the only real moments. Every Thursday I think I will drive on, straight past his house, just to go on seeing and listening. Every Thursday I change down into first to take his steep drive and come to a crunching halt by his nail-studded front door.

One day I will not stop. The little car will do what I ask it. When I reach the Bartley Mill turn-off, I won't take it. I'll keep on towards Lamberhurst, the same sun and shadow rippling over my bonnet like so much water.

In our sitting-room, when I was growing up, there were two chairs: a big, comfortable armchair for my father, and a smaller, lower upholstered chair for my mother. I sat on the floor, or on a shabby pouffe, which they eventually had re-covered in leather.

His chair was next to the fire, with a good view of the television, my mother's chair to the left of it, within reach of his left arm. I would sit anywhere, by my mother, or between them, or in front of them, leaning back against their chairs or their knees, or curled in their laps.

He was hardly ever there. My clearest memories of him are of arrivings or leave-takings. I can see him leaning to wave from the train window as it passed the tip of our garden. I can see myself walking dreamily to meet him on summer evenings, struggling to keep up with his quicker pace as we came back.

He went to work every day on the train, one of a crowd of dark-suited men who travelled mysteriously to the city every morning and came home every evening mysteriously from it. As a small child I would listen for him to go by. 'Here he comes!' I can remember my mother saying. 'Here's Daddy!'

And I would run outside, down to the bottom of the garden, where for a moment I could be close to him. I would climb the wooden fence and wave from a clump of golden rod and Michaelmas daisies taller than I was, and he would pass in a rush of steam and smiles and rolled-up newspapers. And I would climb down slowly and go back in.

He was in bed, I think, or shaving, when I left the house. Often he would run the half-mile or so to the bottom station to catch the up train just after nine. He would come home at about seven, when my mother and I had already eaten, when I had already done most of my homework. At weekends and on special days like Christmas Eve or New Year's Eve he would be out in the evenings too, playing in dance-bands, and he would sleep late the following morning. Then the sounds of the clarinet or the saxophone would rise, never comprehensibly mapping any recognizable melody, always ornate and elusive, rippling from low notes to high and back again without a discernible pattern. When I begged him to play a tune I knew, the results were always disappointing, breathy and flawed. It always ended in the same way: he would complain about the reed and pull down his lower lip to show me the blood-blisters.

His handkerchiefs tell a tale. He gets through about ten a week, their old fabric thin and delicate as muslin with so much wear. And every week I find them stiff as small origami monsters, stuck together with dried mucus in strange configurations. They make a tearing sound as I pull them apart.

Emily has made a mobile of paper cranes. They hang against the light, tipping gently in the draught from the door. They are shaded in rainbow colours – aqua, orange, magenta, blue, gold. Outside the long trailing stems of the Virginia creeper balance in the air, separated from the cranes by glass.

*

10

When people asked me which of my parents I preferred, I always said my father.

My father's handwriting is becoming smaller and smaller. On the old envelope of photographs he sent his mother from the University of Miami it looks enormous. Until you look at it closely, you would think it belonged to someone else.

Here he is in Miami, in 1941, among the grey palm-trees. On the sand, a group of young men are baring their grey knees. Here is the Ford Roadster he was so proud of, parked in front of a University of Miami building with a sun-canopy striped in shades of grey.

Now that my mother is dead, I do my father's laundry. I look out of my kitchen window in October to see sun and shadow dappling his sheets on my line. Somewhere a church clock is striking ten, like a bell tolling somewhere in France. The leaves on the elders are getting thinner and thinner. As they fall, the sky seems to open. The light on the sheets is more and more glaring.

My father made kites, a whole series of them, the flaws of each new model corrected in the next, until that ultimate painted giant rose from the cliff, every bow of its tail folded from a saved chocolate-wrapper, luxurious and glittering.

There are photographs, in black and white: my father's slight figure in baggy trousers, me in a hand-knitted cardigan, my hair in two high bunches. My head is bent with concentration. The wind is blowing my light skirt against the backs of my legs.

Then I am between them as they walk back, holding my hands on either side. I'm pulling sideways towards my mother and hanging my head. I must be sulking, or in disgrace.

I dream I am admiring a new baby. I ask if I may pick her up. At first it is a new-born baby that I am holding in my arms. Then it is an older child which looks strange and rolls its eyes and throws its head and limbs about with sudden jerks. And I am embarrassed that I ever asked to pick it up. Now I'm holding it and I don't know what to do with it. And I won't ever be able to put it back.

Our house was always full of baby stuff, the old wooden play-pen with its toys, bottle-warmers, baby clothes everywhere, Harrington squares draped over chair-arms, teats floating in a saucepan, rugs on the floor strewn with rattles, the wobbly-man policeman that always righted himself on his fat blue base.

These days driving is my greatest pleasure. In my dreams I follow it over and over again, this thin switchback of road between Bells Yew Green and Lamberhurst, always dappled with sun. The larches turn from brown to pale green to darker green, and back to brown again. At the scar where someone was killed in a car accident the commemorative bouquets of flowers fade and disappear, then reappear with the spring. As I drive, there is always a Pyrex casserole of dinner rattling in the back behind me, always a pile of his clean laundry. Sometimes there is a bag of groceries – frozen vegetables and individual fish-steaks and pies and TV dinners for his freezer. Often I bring him fruit – peaches and grapes, satsumas and kiwis and apples. Once, during a particularly grey week in February, I bring him a basket of pink hyacinths just coming into bloom.

One day I shall bring him lunch and the house will be quite quiet. I shall listen for the sound of his keening, and hear only the drip of a tap. I shall go through to the kitchen and turn it off hard. I pick up the crumpled tea-towel and hang it in its rubber suction holder beside the sink.

Then I shall go upstairs to his bedroom. He will be lying in bed, his face turned to the lamp. On the china lamp-base the little koala clings to its mother. Its eyes are closed.

And my father's eyes will be closed. He will look as if he is asleep. From the doorway he will look as if he is smiling.

*

12

When my parents were out together, it was always my father who drove. Even when his sight was bad, just before the cataract operations. My mother would sit quietly beside him and let herself be driven through an invisible fog.

My mother made no secret of the fact that she was a nervous driver. My father would pat her on the knee. 'She's a *wonderful* driver!' he would say. 'She drives perfectly!' He would turn and smile at her. 'When I'm with you and you're driving, I never worry for a moment.'

One day, when I am driving my father to our house for lunch, I hit a bump in the road. The car bounces. We bounce in our seats. 'Oh, Lord!' he says. 'Why do you always drive right in the gutter? You're just like your mother. Joy always used to do that.'

I dream that Bridget and I are in a big, warm, old-fashioned kitchen, making bread. She is at the centre, at some kind of floury, marble-topped table, rolling and kneading something. She is six or seven. I move over to one corner of the room, and as I do I feel a cold draught on my legs, coming from a vent at floor level. I know it is *them*, that they are coming back. I have to concentrate very hard. I have to say things. It is a sort of imprecation – yet not in the tone of a real prayer, or even of a blasphemy – calling on God with a kind of total seriousness without belief. Bridget hears me and looks at me and under-stands. She isn't frightened. She realizes that it is working, that my words and concentration are keeping *them* away. And I'm not frightened either, though that cold air is still there, swirling round my ankles. But I'm getting tired. I don't know how long I can go on. It feels like holding my finger to the hole in the dike.

One Thursday I shall let myself in and he will be in the sitting-room, on his knees. All round him on the floor are photographs – colour snapshots, black and white, brown. Not just pictures of my mother, but pictures of him as a young man in the air force, pictures of me as a baby, pictures of their wedding, and of our own. I shall reach down and pick up the big box of matches he keeps on the hearth. And I shall take the snapshots one by one and burn them in front of his eyes.

My father used to play in a dance-band. Every Friday and Saturday night he would be out, making music for couples to dance to. He would drive back late, in the early hours of the morning, when the country roads were almost deserted. He would come home from Redhill, or Purley or Whiteleafe, or Ashford, or Winchelsea, with a car-load of assorted black cases lined with velvet. He would bring back clarinet, saxophones – tenor and alto – percussion instruments. Sometimes there would be a whole drum-kit. In the front passenger seat he would prop his vibraphone, the graduated metal notes folded with the steel frame in its canvas bag. One night a policeman had stopped him and questioned him about his business. He had answered. Then the constable had poked his head in through the window. 'And who's your passenger?' he had asked him.

My father always laughed when he told this story. And my mother and I would laugh with him, at the unspoken implication – that the 'passenger' was a body, and my father the murderer who was trying to dispose of it, without much success.

He played once in some gala concert in Edenbridge. I can remember his small silhouette as he stood up to play a solo. I don't remember whether he played it well or badly. I had had diarrhoea all day with the thought of it.

When I was about thirteen my father took me to the Fairfield Hall in Croydon to hear Dave Brubeck. 'But don't you want to go?' I remember asking my mother.

'Oh, no. You go. It's not my kind of thing. I can never seem to sit still in concerts. You two go. You'll enjoy it, together.'

And we did enjoy it. We talked about it for years afterwards. 'Do you remember that fantastic drum solo?' we would ask each other. 'The way he improvised . . . ?' And I would remember how I had gone there with him, in my mother's place, how I had seen and heard what she should have been hearing and seeing, how I had crossed the crowded foyer at his elbow, how he had guided me to my seat. The darkness of the auditorium, the light bouncing off the cymbal as it swayed after it had been hit.

'That Pritchard fellow came to see me yesterday morning.'

'Oh. Did he?' I wait for my father to shuffle through the kitchen door towards me. It feels interminable. Several times he stops to rest, supporting himself on the back of a chair, hanging his head. Once he bends down stiffly to pick up a shrivelled frozen pea from the rug. He crouches there for so long without moving that I think he is incapable of getting up. Then finally he manages to stand and balance his single dirty plate on the edge of the draining-board. I take it from him and wash it. 'Did he?' I say again.

'He didn't seem very interested in the home help business.'

'No?'

'He seemed more interested in that lunch-club they run down in the Lion Hall.'

I dry my hands on the tea-towel. 'That might take you out of yourself a bit,' I say carefully.

He stands looking at me.

'Well, don't you feel you could give it a try?'

He grunts. 'I know what he thinks.'

'What? What does he think?'

There is no resentment in his voice, only the same colourless fatigue. 'He thinks if I go to that, I'll be dealt with, sorted out. He won't have to worry about me.'

I want to say, 'I don't suppose he loses too much sleep over you as it is.' Instead I put my arms round him and kiss him on his cheek, just by his ear. I hear myself saying, 'I worry about you. And I love you.' I look over his shoulder at the damp tea-towel still trailing, crumpled, from my fist. 'I worry about you, almost all the time.' I take a deep breath. 'But you never know, you

15

might actually get some pleasure out of meeting new people, talking to someone. They have the same meals-on-wheels lunch, I think. You wouldn't miss your dinner.'

He says with a catch in his voice, 'I don't suppose they would want an old misery like me there.' A tear falls on the plastic tiles. He fumbles for his handkerchief.

I say gently, 'Don't you think you could cheer up a bit for them?'

I leave him and go upstairs to change the sheets on his bed. I pull the covers off and throw them into a heap on the floor with his darned bedsocks and patched pyjamas. His sheets are pieced with ugly, irregular seams, botched on my mother's unresponsive, badly converted treadle. In my hurry I almost get tangled in them as I reach over for the folded clean ones. I put the bottom sheet on and smooth it out over his narrow single bed, the smell of my own fresh laundry rising all round me. Then the old black sock, lumpy and distorted by its content of corks, floating on the empty white like a marker. And suddenly, in spite of anything I can do, the whole bedroom is swimming.

I dream my mother is with me. We are in my father's bedroom. He has fallen out of bed on to the floor. He's asleep in a bundle of eiderdown and blankets.

I think we aren't going to be able to lift him, but somehow we do. We pick him up and put him back in bed and tuck him in gently. He is still asleep. And I think, 'So she *is* real, then, because I couldn't have lifted him on my own.' And then I see John is also there with me, that he is the one who took my father's weight. And I am grateful, even though I'm thinking, 'So she *isn't* real, then, in that sense. She didn't help me lift my father into bed. She is here with us. But it was John who did the lifting.' And I find myself feeling suddenly almost happy. She is there for us, in the way she *can* be. And my father is back in bed, asleep.

The phone rings and I pick up the receiver. 'Mrs Collins?' It is a woman's voice, pleasant. 'You don't know me. I'm Vanessa

Taylor of the Ashdown Social Services. I just wanted to have a word with you about your father.'

I wait, my hand already beginning to shake on the dark grey plastic.

'Mrs Collins?'

'Yes.'

'It's just that it was rather unfortunate. He finally managed to get down to the lunch-club on Tuesday and of course we weren't expecting him and he was rather late and we were just loading up the minibus to go on the outing.'

'Yes?' I say again.

'And, poor man, he'd made such an effort, we couldn't just let him go home, so we twisted his arm and managed to persuade him to come with us. And he came, and I think he enjoyed it, the sea and the lunch and everything. And he's such a charming man, isn't he, and we do so hope he'll come back. You will reassure him and tell him how much we want him to come again, won't you?'

'Yes,' I say. 'Of course.'

'And it really was so unfortunate.' There is a silence at the other end of the line.

'Why?' I say. 'What happened?'

'If we'd known, we'd never have put him at the back, but of course by the time he could get to the door it was too late and he couldn't help it, obviously, and we cleaned him up as well as we could, but we're so worried he may feel embarrassed and not want to come again.'

'I see. Yes. Thanks. I'll talk to him.'

'It really didn't bother us at all, and the other club members were all very understanding.'

'Yes. Thank you. I'll tell him. Of course.' There is a click. The receiver starts to purr gently in my hand.

When I ring him I pretend to know nothing. I only enquire whether he managed to get to the lunch-club at last.

'Oh, yes. We went on a trip to Eastbourne, we had a lovely

17

lunch at a village pub on the way – fish and chips and some sort of gateau. And I had a half of lager. It was all very nice. Everyone was so kind. They all remembered Joy. And next week they're having some sort of entertainment.'

I want to laugh. I say carefully, 'And you didn't feel ill on the bus at all?'

'Oh. Yes,' he says. 'As a matter of fact. Just when we were nearly home. Made a bit of a mess of my new trousers, I'm afraid.'

'Don't worry about that. I can wash them at the weekend. As long as it didn't spoil your day.'

'Oh, no,' he says easily. 'It was just that I've lost one of the handkerchiefs. One of the new ones you just got me. I think they must have used it to . . . you know. And then it got thrown away.'

'Don't worry about that either. I can get you some more.'

He is silent for a moment. Then he says, 'No, you needn't do that for the time being. I think I've got enough to be going on with.'

As I put down the phone, I can feel my face twitching into a smile. The smile becomes a grin. Before I finish loading the dishwasher I am singing.

When I was carsick as a child, my parents would try to keep me from throwing up. 'Tell us when you're just about to be sick.' And my father would stop the car and walk me up and down the road, until I was ready to begin again.

I only had to get into a car to start feeling sick. Just the smell of the upholstery, the close air with its undercurrents of petrol, the sight of my father's hands on the wheel, were enough.

Later, his driving would do it. He would tail slow vehicles with visible impatience, accelerating until he was almost against the other car's back bumper and then dropping back, tapping his fingers on the wheel. Then he would accelerate again. 'What an old worsted woman!' he would say, regardless of the other driver's age or sex.

18

I can see him driving me to an airport once, the minutes ticking away as we followed a horsebox, the horse's rump gleaming in front of us, the top of its dark tail. 'I can't take this,' I said to him. 'Every time you go to pass, my heart is really pounding!'

He took his eyes from the road to stare at me. 'What do you mean, your heart's pounding?'

'I mean it's going "thump, thump" in my chest. I wish you wouldn't try to overtake on these country roads. I'm scared. I'd rather miss the plane.'

'It doesn't do your heart any harm to thump,' he said.

My father drove us to our wedding. About a hundred yards from the house there was a car parked on the other side of the road. A van was coming down the hill towards us. It drew out to overtake the car. I willed my father to slow down and let it go.

But he didn't. He put his foot down harder. The two vehicles drew up with a crunch, nose to nose. Then we just sat there. The two drivers glared. In a minute they would get out and start shouting at each other. But my father didn't give an inch. We waited. The seconds ticked by. The seconds became minutes. The flowers in my lap seemed to wilt. Then the driver of the van went slowly into reverse, scowling, muttering obscenities. We drove off without an acknowledgement.

Then my father grunted. 'Well. It wasn't his right of way. It was mine.'

When I was a little girl I had a recurring dream about a car. It wasn't an ordinary car. It was a small go-kart of a car that travelled low on the ground, buzzing like a dangerous insect. I would be walking on the pavement outside our house and I would hear it coming up behind me.

After these dreams I would wake up sweating, struggling to run against a tangle of bedclothes. I knew it would get me. I could still hear it in the dark, buzzing nearer and nearer.

But one night I worked out what to do. As soon as I heard it coming up behind me, I turned round. I lay down on the ground in front of it and it ran right over me. Then I stood up and walked away.

'How was the club on Tuesday?'
    He looks up at me and blinks before replying. 'Oh. All right.'
    'Did you do anything interesting?'
    'No, I don't think so. Not that I can remember. Did you?'
    'Did I what?'
    'Do anything interesting.'
    'Well, actually . . .' I lean back in my chair. 'I won – '
    'Oh, yes!' He interrupts me. 'If you go into the other room and look on the sofa you'll see something.'
    I get up and manoeuvre myself through the resistant sliding doors. The sofa is almost covered with piles of old newspapers. But at one end, on a bare patch of upholstery, there are three small bags of chocolate buttons. I come back with them in my hand. 'Do you mean these?'
    'Yes. I won them in the raffle on Tuesday. I thought the girls might like them.'
    'That's very sweet of you. I'm sure they wouldn't say no.'
    He gestures to me to hand him the little bags of sweets and starts looking at them intently, turning them over and peering at the picture and the list of ingredients. 'Perhaps I might like them,' he says.
    'Oh, yes,' I tell him quickly. 'If you fancy them at all yourself, don't . . .'
    'Perhaps I'll just send them one each and keep one.'
    'They aren't very big. Why don't you keep two?'
    He looks up at me like a child. 'Perhaps I will.'
    I take the third packet from him as he holds it out to me. I put the first two back on the sofa, between the newspapers. Then, when I am sure he is not looking at me, I hide the third on the mantelpiece, behind the clock.

One day I will find him sitting in front of the television, eating Smarties. The gas fire is on and I smell the warm rubber from the soles of his slippers. There is a little smear of chocolate like a serif on his chin.

'Where did you get those?' I ask him.

He looks at me almost aggressively. 'I won them. Last Tuesday.'

'You won them?' I repeat blankly. 'How?'

'At the lunch-club. In the raffle.'

On the screen an episode of some soap opera is coming to an end. A young, brittle-looking woman doctor strides out of the ward office, her hands thrust deep into the pockets of her white coat.

'In the raffle,' he says. He holds out the tube to me. 'Do you want one?'

'I don't want to rob you,' I say.

'It's all right. I've got plenty.'

'What do you mean?'

His eyes are twinkling.

'In the bedroom. Go up and look.'

And I will shrug and go upstairs, to humour him. And when I open the door, I shan't be able to believe it. Not just cereal packets, but packets and tins and jars of everything. Not just Corn Flakes and Rice Krispies, but red salmon and baked beans and guava halves in syrup, macaroni and lentils and paper napkins, boxes and boxes of chocolates, crackers, shortbread, a woman's purse made of mock sealskin, a gift basket of assorted bath cubes.

I go downstairs to where the white end-titles are swimming up from the bottom of the screen. 'Where did it all come from?' I ask.

'From the club. I won it all in the raffle. I told you.' He holds out the tube of Smarties to me again, and this time I take one.

'I think you'd better start trying to lose,' I say drily.

This first year we are brave enough, or silly enough, to take my father on holiday with us to France. We are highly organized. We help him to pack his case and bring him back to our house, to be ready for an early start the next morning. He needs a good hour and a half to prepare himself and have breakfast, to clean his teeth and empty his bowels while we all wait. We set the alarm for five.

But something goes wrong: I wake at six to a radio-alarm that is still silent. I jump out of bed, exclaiming.

We bundle ourselves into the little car, the girls still half asleep, my father too confused to protest. As we rocket through Tonbridge towards the M20, I struggle to put in my contact lenses, but it is too soon. The sterilizing solution isn't properly neutralized. My eyes sting and tears stream down my face. I fumble to take the lenses out again. We are packed in the back, the girls and I, like sardines. John drives to Ramsgate fast. On the boat I have no difficulty persuading him to join us in the big breakfast he swore he would never want.

It is a long, hot, two-day journey down through France. By the time we reach our small hotel my father is feeling faint and dizzy. My head aches with the anxiety. These days every time he complains I wonder if he is dying.

But in the evening we sit out in a courtyard to eat, by a little fountain lit from underneath, white lights swimming in its bowl. The girls dabble their hands. When my father has gone to bed, I smoke a cigarette under the stars. Two years later he will still reminisce about this place, the salmon in pastry, the warm dusk, the music of the water. He will still remember it, when many other things are forgotten.

For him the old farmhouse must be full of memories of my mother. For me it is also full of the children, eight years younger – Emily in her red American cotton dress, perched on the huge stone window-sills, Bridget in a baby's sun-hat playing with Lego bricks and a plastic bowl of water in the shade of an outhouse.

I want us to eat our dinner outside. We drag the table out on to the grass. For me, this is one of the good things France has to offer: warm peaches, warm wine, cheeses going liquid on the plate as you lean back in your chair and look at the hills. But it is too hot. It is too hot for my father. In the end it is too hot for us.

One day we visit Vézelay. After a long warm drive we are finally standing on that hill, in that cool space with its carvings and grey-chequered arches. Bridget asks me in a whisper if we can stay all day, and I say I hope so. I could sit here for several hours and still not want to go home.

But my father won't go right into the church. I catch him looking sideways at the nuns and priests and tourists, as if they belonged to some dark cult. He parks himself with his tripod on a bench by the door and closes his eyes. After less than half an hour he has waylaid Emily to give me a message. He wants to know how soon we can go back. When we decide to cut our losses and walk down to the car again, he makes me promise not to visit any more old churches. He makes it sound like a perversion.

I dream my father is an elephant, a small elephant. As we watch, they lead him out and string him up between two trees. And then they tighten the ropes until the bones of his front legs and his hind legs crack and break. I can hear them cracking. And then they cut him down and somehow he still stands on his hind legs, his little broken forelegs dangling, too long for his body. So they chop off his front feet to make them shorter, like a butcher cutting a chop with a cleaver. Once. Twice. Until they are the right length. Then they lead him away, and when they bring him gently back, he is my father, with his bloody stumps all bandaged. And he seems to be unaware of it all, only complaining of his slowness and dizziness in his usual voice.

One afternoon I can't stand it any longer. I can't bear just sitting in the farmhouse kitchen waiting for my father to cry. It is raining. 'Put your macs on,' I say to Emily and Bridget. 'Let's go for a walk.'

We dress up in waterproofs and set off down the lane. The lane becomes a track. The ruts are filled with clay-coloured water, grasses floating in them like hair. Our feet squelch. The hems of our jeans are dragging with wet. The rain goes on falling, harder and harder. The grey curtain blows at us across fields and hedges without a break. We try to step round puddles and find ourselves ankle-deep in mud. It is hopeless. Then I slip and fall over. The front of my jacket is covered with dirt. I've ripped my trousers at the knee. My daughters are trying not to laugh.

'Let's sing,' I say. They look at me. And we start to bellow out songs, folk-songs, Guide songs, Christmas carols, anything. We shout the words at the rain. We make up a new song with a nonsense chorus and shout it into the dripping leaves. The girls' faces are pink, the hair clinging to their cheeks in dark wisps. The piece of torn fabric at my knee flaps to and fro like a wet flag.

My father had his spine broken during the war, in a road accident in North Africa. Since then his back has always given trouble. A succession of problems, sciatica and slipped discs, recurred periodically to keep him in bed, flat on his back. He had a strange garment, something between a corset and a liberty bodice, that he would put on under his clothes whenever he was expecting to have to lift something.

Once they put him in plaster, his whole trunk encased in a hard white shell. When you hugged him it felt like hugging a wall.

He would tell us the story of how he was on the tube, one evening in the rush-hour, next to a – presumably attractive – young woman, squashed helplessly against her ribs. And how she glared at him with something like outrage as he thrust his hard, muscled torso against her with an insistence that could only be described as provocative. I loved my father when he told me this story.

My father has lost his cap, the tweed and corduroy cap he always wears in the car, even when the weather is at its hottest. 'I wish I could find my cap,' becomes his daily greeting to all of us.

One morning I am just finishing breakfast in the big, cool-tiled kitchen when I hear him scratching and tugging at the farmhouse door. I go to open it for him. Sun streams in across the stone steps, the dead grass and pale breadcrumbs on the red floor. He is standing there in a blaze of light, smiling.

My first thought is that he is ill. My first thought is that he must be dying. Why else would he smile? 'What is it? What's the matter?' I ask him.

He doesn't answer me. He just stands there with that odd grin on his face.

'What's the matter? Are you all right?'

Then he grunts. 'You're not very observant.'

'What?'

And he points to his head, with a kind of triumph. 'My cap! Didn't you notice? I found it!'

I want to cry with relief. I find myself looking past him at the sunlit grass, smelling the sap. A single grasshopper sets up its electric whirr. I blink. Once. Twice. I reach out and take the cap gently from his head. 'You clever old thing,' I tell him.

One particularly airless afternoon we are just about to go out to stock up with groceries. As we try to work out what we need, clouds start to come up over the brow of the hill. The sky gets darker. Then, quite suddenly, the wind rises. It catches at deckchairs, blows the lid off the rubbish and sends the bin rolling. We run round grabbing everything and pulling it back into shelter. We lean on the door to close it against the wind and find ourselves, all four, in the end bedroom, next to the room where my father is still resting.

For half an hour the wind pounds us. Outside things rattle and crash and splinter, but the wind itself almost drowns them. For the girls' sake I hide my nervousness. Then quite suddenly the wind drops and we walk outside to look at the damage. The garage-barn has had half its roof torn off, the grass in front of it is covered with fragments of slipped tile. John drags a branch out of the road. Our kitchen roof has a huge hole in it, above the stove. From inside you can look up and see the sky. The newer farmhouse opposite and the house in the lane have sustained the same kind of damage. Within minutes we find ourselves in a little voluble crowd talking of *tornade, assurances, réparations*.

That night I think my father is almost happy. We cook and eat by candlelight, joking. Bridget wanders round in a red plastic mac and construction worker's helmet we find on a shelf. She shines the torch in our faces. We eat a good meal, all of us. And my father is happy. It must be the Blitz spirit. Or else he has brought us all to the place where he already is, where roofs naturally splinter and gape with unmendable holes.

My father was always 'brainy'. 'Oh, yes,' my mother would say proudly, teasing him. 'Eric *Wicks*! Matriculating at fifteen!'

And he would take her cue and boast, 'I took the scholarship a year early, to the grammar school. Second in Surrey! They put me in the class above Ted, even though he was two years older!' He would laugh drily. 'He never got over it!'

'And after that? What happened then?' I would ask him. 'When you matriculated? What did you do then?'

'Higher Schools,' he would say. 'Maths. Sciences. But I don't know.' He would shake his head. 'A bit dry, all that.'

And my mother would smile. 'He started playing in bands,' she said. 'That's what it was. He got in with Ted's crowd. All he wanted to do was to save up and get a car.' And then she would lean over to me and whisper, 'And he was frightened of doing too well, in case it meant he had to leave his mother!'

The rivalry between my father and his elder brother, Ted, was always intense. My father always implied that he had a better job than Ted, even though Ted was older and taller. My father never let us forget that when I was only five he had bought his own house, while the house Ted and Ivy and their two children lived in in Merstham was only rented.

One day, shortly after his seventy-ninth birthday, my father says to me, 'You know, it makes me feel strange.'

26

'What does?' I ask him.

'Being seventy-nine.'

It doesn't seem like that much of a landmark. 'What do you mean?' I say.

'Well . . .' He hesitates. 'Because of my brother. Ted died when he was seventy-eight. I suppose I'm outliving him.'

I stare. He actually chuckles. 'I suppose I'm doing better than he did.'

My mother met my father playing tennis. It was a family joke. One evening she had confided in her sister, Mona, 'Do you know, I think I may be falling for Eric Wicks.'

And my aunt had said, in disbelief, 'Eric Wicks? *No!?*'

My mother had a little dog, a dachshund called Lindy. It had a weak heart. It was quite stupidly attached to her. If ever she was ill, the silly creature would refuse to go out. My father or I would have to drag it down the street by the lead, its short legs scrabbling to resist us, its belly grazing the pavement until we turned for home.

The day my parents came to tell me Lindy had had to be put down I was out collecting frogspawn with my cousin. 'What do you mean, her stomach turned over?' I must have frowned as I tried to imagine it.

'Like a paper bag. You know how they do it at the green-grocer's? Like that.'

'Couldn't they have given her an operation to turn it back?'

'She was too old, darling. Her heart wouldn't have stood it.'

I thought about that. About what having a weak heart meant. About the brown paper bag full of peas or Brussels sprouts, that twisted at the corners and couldn't be untwisted, so that nothing in it could ever get out. About the jars of frogspawn with the string handles tied at their necks, the way the slimy eggs had slithered and flopped between our wet fingers.

*

Sometimes when my mother was exasperated with my father she would say, half laughing, 'Even a worm turns, you know!'

In her child-care book there were old-fashioned black and white photographic illustrations. Among the rashes – measles, German measles, chicken pox, scarlet fever – there was a picture of worms. Life-size, the legend said. A round-worm that stretched the vertical length of the page, a tapeworm that reached right to the bottom margin and curled back again slightly towards the top.

In one of his old magazines I see an advertisement. It is for something called a Lifeline, an alarm system for people who live alone and who are disabled or infirm.

In the photograph a well-dressed elderly woman is lying on a carpet. The telephone is just out of her reach. Her cardigan is buttoned, her skirt covers her knees discreetly. Her perfectly waved hair has just been combed and patted into place. Something about the self-consciousness of her expression as she looks up at the camera reminds me of my mother.

'What about one of these?' I ask him. 'Wouldn't you be glad of one of these?' I point to the woman in the picture. 'Look, you could have a fall, and not be able to contact anyone. If you had one of these Lifeline things, you could press a button and I'd know you were in trouble.'

He grunts. He doesn't say yes. He doesn't say no. He studies the photograph for several minutes. Then he grunts again. 'I suppose you could find out how much these things cost.'

Sometimes I would ask my mother why they never had any more children. She would say carefully, 'We didn't have enough money, darling.' And I would think of other families, where children grew like weeds, and seemed to thrive, where the air they grew up breathing wasn't anxiety, but something more ordinary.

I was thirteen when I first went to France for three weeks to stay with Arlette and her family. Every night at dinner I ate a banana, because my nails were bitten to the quick and I was too embarrassed to try to peel an orange. Soon I got constipated. I wrote a tear-stained letter to my mother.

A few days later her reply came, oddly battered and lumpy in its envelope. When I opened it, something fell out. Powder. Fragments. Only one of the Senokot tablets she'd sent me was still in one piece, a web of complicated hairline fractures, a baby snail in its crushed shell.

My first day at infant school seemed so long. The morning itself was more than long enough. At lunch-time we all stood with our hands together and prayed. 'Now you can all go home,' Miss Harkness said.

I think I forgot everything. I forgot everything my parents had ever told me. I couldn't see my cousin anywhere. I slipped out of the school gate and started to walk.

With my head down, I walked home as fast as I could. It was over a mile. I wasn't yet five. I was only just old enough to find my way home.

I reached the big Victorian house on the edge of the village, where we lived in our upstairs flat. I stood at the front door, my back to the road and to the fields and woods beyond. I made my hand into a fist and pounded, as high up as I could reach.

I can remember my mother coming to the door, standing in the open doorway, the look of consternation on her face. 'Darling!' she must have said.

'They told us to come home now.'

'But it's only dinner-time! You were supposed to stay and have dinner at school. You knew that. Didn't you remember?'

'They told us to come home,' I said again. 'So I came home. I can have dinner at home with you.'

'But, sweetheart, I'm not having anything for dinner. I haven't got anything for you. I'm only having a boiled egg.'

'I like boiled eggs. Please.' I was in tears. 'Let me stay and have a boiled egg with you.'

She looked at me anxiously, hesitating. Then her eyes strayed to something beyond me, something behind me on the road. I heard a car door slam. And suddenly Miss Harkness was there, her arm round me as she crouched on the gravel to talk to me. She looked up at my mother. 'I'm so sorry! It must have been my fault.' She smiled. 'I took my eyes off her for just a second, and when I looked round, she was gone.' She took my hand and led me back towards the car. I let her help me in. I let her dry my eyes. 'Blow!' she said. Then, 'It's all right, little one.' I let her hug me and sit me on her knee.

I find myself collecting mountains, as other people collect photographs. Mont Blanc, Mont d'Or, Aiguille du Midi, Monte Cinto, Mount Rainier, Bighorns, Blue Ridge, Grand Tetons. Grand Tetons. It is a female mythology we have almost in our blood, from the sentimental red sunsets of *Heidi* – old age, sickness, blindness, beauty, freedom. Every mountain landscape I find myself in is a ledge I shall eventually push my father over. Where I shall watch his wheelchair bucketing down over rocks and challenge him to stand on his own feet.

Sometimes I would ask my parents why they never had any other children. They would look at me and smile, puzzled. 'But you were enough for us, darling. We never wanted anyone but you.'

He goes to stay a week with an old friend in Wiltshire. John drives him down, and drives back a week later to collect him. The day he gets back I ring him in the evening. 'Well,' I say. 'Did you have a good time? How did it go?'

'Oh, fine.' He hesitates. 'Helen was very sweet. She looked after me wonderfully. We went to see – you know who I mean – Dilys who used to live next door. She gave us a lovely tea. Scones and home-made jam.'

'You mean next door to Helen?'

'Yes. Isn't that what I said?'

I ignore this. 'You'll be able to give me a blow-by-blow account when I come over on Thursday.' I want to reassure him, to reassure us both. 'And how are you feeling now?'

'Oh, fine,' he says again. 'Fine. If only I could get my wretched jacket off.'

'What do you mean, get your jacket off? Why can't you get your jacket off? What's wrong with you?' I don't quite manage to keep the panic out of my voice. 'John told me you got back hours ago. Have you been trying all this time?'

'Oh, no. Only for the last half-hour or so.'

'*Half an hour?*'

'It's just that my arm doesn't seem to be working properly.'

It takes me a few seconds to digest this. Then I say awkwardly, 'Look, we obviously can't leave you to go to bed in your jacket, can we? But John's gone swimming and I haven't got the car. I can't do anything till he gets back. I'll talk to him when he comes in and ring you back in about twenty minutes, OK?'

His faint 'Yes' comes to me as if across an immeasurable distance, the last gasp of some small animal, mortally injured. I put down the phone.

Twenty minutes later I ring him again. I count the double tones. Forty. Forty-five. Fifty. I put down the receiver.

There are cars passing in the distance. Somewhere they sweep the road with sound and light. When you cross, they are always stopped. The drivers' faces register boredom, irritation, tolerance. The little green man bleeps and beckons, and they can't hear it. As they drive away, they can still see you in their mirrors. They see you walking. They see the light change back to red.

There is no light visible in the house, but when I unlock the front door I hear voices coming from upstairs. It takes me a moment to realize it is the television. Then he calls out, 'Hello? Is someone there?'

'It's only me.'

I run upstairs and find him sitting on the edge of the bed in his shirt and underpants, watching the flickering blue picture as he strains to pull off a sock. On the screen a New York cop leans forward across a desk in a halo of harsh lamplight. 'You can turn this rubbish off if you like.'

'It's all right. You're watching it.'

He stares at the screen for a moment. Someone crouches behind the hood of a car in an underground parking-lot and holds out a gun, two-handed. 'It was kind of you to come and see me.'

'That's all right. I was worried when you didn't answer the phone. Didn't you hear it ring?'

'No. I didn't hear anything.'

'Anyway, you got your jacket off all right.'

'Yes. Yes. It was a bit of a struggle. My arm's a bit sore.'

'A bit sore?'

'From when I fell out of bed last night. I think I've dislocated my elbow.'

'*What?*'

'Dislocated my elbow.'

'Is it swollen?' I ask him. 'Can you bend it normally?'

'Well . . . I *can* . . . but it feels a bit sore. And my leg.'

'What's wrong with your leg?'

'You have a look at it.' He stands up. His legs are pitifully thin, bent as a cartoon jockey's. The gap between his knees must be a good six inches. 'Do you see it?'

'What? Where?'

He points to a place just below his left hip and I turn him gently as I would a child until I can see where he means. There is a blurred red mark there, a few inches across, that could be a pressure-mark. 'Do you see it?'

'It looks as if you've given yourself a bruise,' I say.

I hug him and go downstairs to make him a hot drink, warming the milk in his mug in the microwave. Over the ragged music and American voices from the TV I hear his high wail start up, change tone like a siren, hang in the night somewhere above me.

*

I arrange to have a phone put in on our first-floor landing. I am afraid it will ring at night and I won't be able to get to it in time.

I dream I am in bed with John. We are just about to have sex. Then for some reason we stop and get up, and I start to strip the bed and fold up the sheets. As I shake them, a big bug plops out on to the floor. I look up and the whole room is crawling. They are swarming at the edges of the dormer window. The walls and ceiling are black.

I go downstairs to the ground floor. The front door is standing open and people are coming in, laughing, with drinks in their hands. There are bright lights everywhere, amplifiers, wires snaking across the floor. A band is tuning up in the kitchen. And the kitchen wall has been knocked down, so our house is open to next door. Our whole street is one enormous party.

One winter my father's back was worse than usual. Someone brought a bed downstairs to the sitting-room and made it up for him. And he would lie there under the beams and the flickering firelight while our lives went on round him.

I crawled under the covers and asked him to tell me stories.

'What do you want me to tell stories about?'

'Tell me about bombs,' I would say.

And he would tell me in detail everything he had learned in the RAF and from newspapers, and from simply living through the war: how the planes dropped their dark loads over Germany to explode on impact, how a bomb could fall and wait with a clock ticking quietly inside it, how the flying bombs were never anything to worry about, so long as you could still hear the engine.

There was the V1 that my grandmother saw passing the church spire, the time she hid under the kitchen table. The explosion took out the house opposite, showering her with broken glass and plaster, making her Surrey cottage precarious and uninhabitable. There was the flash my father stood to witness at the window one night in Edenbridge, as he waited for the crash that would shake my sleeping mother from her bed.

But best of all was the unexploded mine, the huge metal egg they cradled so gently in scaffolding and defused, a miracle of courage and steady hands, like some dangerous game of pick-a-sticks for adults.

'Tell me about bombs,' I would beg him.

He would smile tolerantly from his sick-bed. 'What, again?'

And I would nod silently.

And he would tell it to me again.

Now, whenever I visit my father, his Lifeline button is on the table beside his place-mat. He never seems to wear it.

'Why don't you hang it round your neck?' I ask him. 'Or clip it on to your pocket? If you get up to go to the loo, or into the kitchen, that's when you could fall. It doesn't make sense to leave it behind.'

'Oh . . .' He frowns. 'I did wear it once. When I was feeling particularly dizzy. But I leaned on it by accident, and then this woman came on. "Mr Wicks, are you all right?" So I thought I'd better not wear it again.'

'I'm sure she didn't say it like that!'

He smiles faintly.

The next time I come to visit him I notice he has left the Lifeline button upstairs, on the bathroom window-sill.

Everything my father ever made was special. When I was small my parents rented an upstairs flat in a big old Victorian house on the edge of the village. But we had the use of a garden. In the garden my father built me a swing. I was barely five when we left there, but I still remember every feature of that swing: the heavy posts treated with creosote, embedded in concrete; the wiry hairs of the ropes under my hands; the smooth wooden seat he needed a spirit-level to adjust.

It was a permanent fixture of that first garden. I was in tears as we drove away. But my father could do anything. When the removal lorry drew up at the new house, I screamed with delight. There was the swing, perched on top of our pile of tea-chests and shabby furniture. My father was grinning at me. The creosoted legs stuck out from the heap, still encased in their concrete boots.

My father made me stilts. They weren't like the stilts you could buy, which were almost impossible to master. They were real, usable stilts that extended right up behind your shoulder-blades so you could balance. They made me about two feet taller. I learned to walk on them forwards, backwards, sideways, over astonishing distances.

'Can you pack your own things?' I shall ask him.

There won't be any answer.

'Are you capable of packing your own things?'

But he will be staring at nothing, his jaw slack and wordless. When I touch his cheek, his skin will be cold against the back of my hand. I shall hug him and he will half smile. I shall reach under his bed and pull out his biggest suitcase, the soft-topped one they bought to go to France. I shall begin to fill it with his clothes, the old shirts with the tucks to shorten the sleeves, the darned bedsocks, the old man's front-button vests with their changed geography of holes. 'I've got some new inners,' he will say.

'What?'

He will wave his hand at the suede lace-ups I'm holding, and he will articulate very clearly: 'In the little drawer in the wardrobe. Some new inners I bought for those.'

Inside the shoes, under the blotched suede, something is grey and curled at the edges. I shall lift them to my nose and sniff, but they will have no recognizable smell. Nothing about him really smells any more. I shall have a sudden visual memory of my mother, snipping round a new pair of inner-soles with kitchen scissors, shaving them to his size, the soft white crescent of foam rubber dangling from the blades. 'Put them in the case,' I shall tell him. 'I'll cut them down for you as soon as we get there.'

As he struggles to raise himself from where he is sitting on the edge of the bed, I am already filling the case with piles of pullovers, trousers, towels. His corduroy and wool cap will sit on the top, folded into itself like an oyster.

Before the kids come in we shall be on the road. He will be sitting beside me in his scarf and sun-glasses, his whole body slightly out of true, as if he is too weak to manoeuvre himself into a more comfortable position. As the traffic bunches and eases on the M25, I shall tap my fingers on the wheel. His wheel. I have taken his car. Once I shall find myself glancing at him out of the corner of my eye, expecting to see him slumped, or drawn, the skin at the corner of his eyes snagged into a pattern of helpless endurance. But he will be sitting up straight, his head up to meet the unrolling of the road, his eyes behind the dark glasses as quick as a bird's.

When we turn off on to the M40, something will seem to change. As the traffic thins out and the road opens in front of us, he will start to talk to me. 'Of course, this road wasn't even here, the time Joy and I . . .' His voice will falter, and I shall think he is going to cry, but he will pass over it and go on. 'We towed the little van all the way up, to a little site right up in the mountains. The sheep used to come and look at us through the windows. I remember . . .'

I shall glance sideways at him again, but he will go on.

'I remember we had the door open one morning, and Joy was cooking the bacon and she heard a sound right behind her, like a sneeze. She said, "Are you all right, darling?" and when she turned round there was a sheep standing there just behind her back, poking its head in through the door!'

There will be tears in his eyes, but he will be laughing as he remembers.

'Not much of a compliment to you,' I shall say.

And soon we'll be driving between fields and half-wooded valleys. We'll turn north-west and the hills will unfold in front of us, layer on layer. As we come down towards the sea, the sun will be full in our eyes, turning our windscreen white and opaque as milk.

*

36

With a builder friend of his, my father made us a garage. It grew up complete with an extra toilet and a workshop for himself. He would spend long Saturday afternoons in there, 'poking around'. In front there was a flower-bed, which was nominally mine, and a soakaway which flooded regularly every time there was a downpour. We all knew the exact depth of the hardcore, and the exact time it had taken to dig the hole and fill it in.

My mother couldn't sleep at night. She took sleeping-pills every evening, but still she woke up in the early hours and came downstairs to knit or read. Or she would sit in a chair, watching the sky lighten over the grey fields, and think. She would write little notes to me then.

When my mother told me about the personal dynamics of her bridge circle, she would exude a special kind of intelligence. She would frown slightly as she explained. Sometimes she would laugh. Nothing, not the faintest 'atmosphere', escaped her. She could always trace it back to where it began. But she always wanted reassurance from my father and me. Replaying the scene and her small appeaser's part in it, she always wanted our approval. 'You don't think she could possibly have been hurt by that?' she would ask. 'You don't think I was being interfering?'

After my Uncle Harry's retirement, he and my aunt moved to a little house barely a quarter of a mile from my parents'. My mother was so excited. 'Do you know what?' she greeted me breathlessly one day. Her eyes were shining. Her cheeks were pinker than usual. 'Mona's coming to live in Deepdene! Mona and Harry are buying a house just down the lane! I can't believe it!'

But the two sisters hardly saw each other. They never met regularly for tea or coffee. They both had husbands. There would be barely time for a hug and a few questions. Sometimes a jar of marmalade or a bag of tomatoes would change hands. Then, 'I mustn't stop, Harry's in the car,' they would say, or, 'You know what Eric's like.'

As far as I know, there is only one childhood photo of the three sisters together. They are sitting on a fence. Ruby, the eldest, who was sent to live with the grandmother, her long thin black-stockinged legs reaching almost to the ground. Mona slightly boyish under the page-boy haircut. The two little ones sitting close together, like two small birds.

A luminous morning. Clear sky, trees almost bare now. Look at them quickly out of the corner of your eye and you catch yourself thinking it is spring.

Somehow I manage to leave my father and fly to the United States for a month to write. Up to the very last moment he half threatens to have a stroke, and I half believe him. One day he actually asks me, 'What will happen if I have a stroke while you're in America?'

'It depends what kind of stroke,' I say. I paint a picture of a vague unease, followed by some slight stiffness in his little finger. I try to laugh. Then I look at him seriously. 'You know I'll come if you ever need me. But try not to want me to. Please.'

When we went to live in Wisconsin for that year, it was my mother who fought against our going. 'You know I won't come and see you in America? You know that, don't you?'

'I don't see why you shouldn't come,' I said. 'You could have a real holiday with us. It would be fun for us to show you everything.'

She shook her head. 'We won't come.'

'Why not?'

'It's such a lot of money, darling.'

'But Auntie Mo's giving you the money. She thinks you should come. She thinks you should jump at the chance.'

'No. I won't go on a plane again.'

I sighed. 'I'm sure Dr Philbert could give you something to make you feel less . . .'

'It's my ears. I can't face it.'

'But the cabins are all pressurized these days,' I told her. 'I'm sure it wouldn't be that bad.'

But for once my mother's expression was almost grim. 'We're not coming. If you decide to go, there won't be any question of seeing us. I want you to be quite clear about that.'

'Well . . .' I must have shrugged. 'It's a pity. You'd enjoy it. But we can write to each other. A year isn't very long . . .'

In my last two years at junior school I suffered from friendships. One intimate friend of mine would bite and scratch; another had created a triangle of jealousies. After a nearly sleepless night I was in my father's bed.

'Don't worry, darling.' His arm was round me as he hugged me. 'You'll have a friend, one day. The kind of friend you deserve.'

I wondered how he knew. I wondered if he knew everything that would happen to me, once I got to the grammar school. 'How do you know?' I asked him. 'What will she be like?'

He thought for a moment. 'She'll have blue eyes.'

'The same colour as mine?'

'Not quite. A bit bluer.'

'And what colour hair?' I said.

'Fair. Fairer than yours. And a nice smile.'

I thought about this. 'How will I know when I meet her?'

He laughed. 'Oh . . . You'll know. She'll be different. There won't be any of this fighting and crying nonsense. She'll look at you and you'll feel like laughing. And you'll know.'

I open the blinds on all the five windows of this room, and look out on to sun. It is just coming up between the tree-branches. There are still some leaves – yellow and brown, maple. The winter is not as far advanced as I expected.

*

Certain nights of the year were our nights, the nights my mother and I shared. My father was always out, playing his music. She and I would sit together in front of the television to watch the last night of the Proms, lifted together on a surge of unlikely patriotism, our eyes full of tears. Or on New Year's Eve we would watch Andy Stewart and the white-skirted dancers with their plaid sashes. Halfway through we would look at each other. 'Shall we turn this off?' And we would nod to each other and grin.

Christmas Eve was the best. He would always be out. The tree was always lit up, its tarnished glass balls winking, collected over the years. Rapt, we would sit through the King's College Chapel service in black and white, to its end. Then we would look at each other and sigh. She would pour us each a single glass of non-alcoholic ginger wine. Later it would be sherry. We would glance at each other sideways, and one of us would say, 'Do you think it would matter if we started on the nuts?'

Sunset through tree-branches. Just this shallow angle of roof with its drift of dry leaves, and then beyond, that huge tree with the dark limbs sweeping down towards the ground.

I dream I am on a blind date. I am meeting someone in a tea-room like that old-fashioned tea-room on the Pantiles. And when I go in, the person who is sitting there waiting to meet me is my mother.

We have tea together. We talk about my father. She is so concerned about him. 'Poor Eric . . .' In the dream the tears come to my eyes.

But when I wake up, I am almost singing.

The squirrels playing in the trees are astonishing. They hang and drop, jump up, streak back along branches, taking such risks. They are a part of the tree. They are the part of the tree that moves.

*

My mother, like most of her wartime generation, was a great collector. She would write lists on pieces of cardboard cut from cereal packets. She would save rubber bands, and pieces of string. She would unravel sweaters and wash out the wool in hanks, to use it again. She would save polythene bags. Her cutlery-drawer was still half full of meat-skewers and plastic scoops from Cow & Gate tins. She would rinse out milk-bottle tops and margarine tubs. She had little boxes full of used stamps.

All night I hear the freight trains crossing this moonlit landscape. Their tracks stretch out across the Midwest, across America. The full moon shines on my window so directly that at first I think it is already morning.

Sitting at our kitchen table for lunch, my mother would pour out her news, and I would pour out mine. My father's eyes would stray to the back window. 'Does that fence belong to you?' he would say, or 'Has your gutter always had that leak?'

When they left, the house would seem to close in on me, its paintwork flaking and seedy, its thin glass cracking in top corners, the whole edifice a mess of rotten fence-panels and defective guttering. I would make myself do something practical for John and the kids. Half an hour later I would look out of the window. The angle of the leaning fence would be scarcely visible under its tangle of roses. Really the drip from the gutter was almost restful.

No one can believe how slow he is now. One morning my mother's sister, Mona, and her husband, Harry, agree to sit with him. When I get back, the three of us go downstairs. My aunt looks at me as if she is in shock. 'He went to the lavatory while you were gone,' she tells me. 'Do you know how long it took him?'

I shake my head.

'*Twenty-five minutes!* And then over half an hour to brush his teeth afterwards! I timed him on my watch.'

I smile.

'He's got *so slow*. It's unbelievable. We didn't realize.'

When we came back from our year in Wisconsin, my father and my Uncle Harry were at Gatwick to meet us. They both looked older than I remembered. We made our way out of the arrivals area, towards the car-park. We stepped out of the lift, confronted by rows of cars. 'They're next to each other, just down here.' Uncle Harry led the way.

We reached the spot. Two strange cars were parked where the Fiesta and Nova ought to have been. 'That's funny.' My father rubbed his chin. 'I could have sworn this was the right place.'

We moved on. 'Perhaps it was the next row,' my Uncle Harry said.

But in the next row a metallic Saab gleamed at the side of a red Maestro. The two elderly men stood and stared, their heads close together, defeated. They turned to look at each other. Then my father said, 'You don't think they could *both* have been stolen?'

One evening I ring his sister, Dorothy. 'He's so slow,' I tell her. 'We're all tearing our hair. You wouldn't believe it!'

But at the other end of the line she chuckles. 'Oh, yes, I *would* believe it! He was always like that. Even when he was young. Do you know, once, when he was quite a young man, he had a week's holiday, and he offered to put up some tiles for my mother, over the sink. About ten tiles. And do you know how long it took him?'

I make a generous guess. 'Two days?'

She splutters. 'A week! That's how long it took him. Ten tiles. It drove us round the bend. The whole week!'

'Well, he always was a perfectionist,' I say drily. 'That's what my mum would call him.'

'Your mum was a sweetheart,' Dorothy says. 'She never said anything mean about anyone.'

*

My father's younger sister, Dorothy, was born on my Uncle Ted's tenth birthday. One day my grandmother was out walking with her three children. A friend stopped to look into the pram.

'Oh, what a beautiful baby! She's so adorable!' She looked at Ted. 'Aren't you a lucky boy to have such a lovely little sister for a birthday present?'

I can see Ted smiling with pride. Then she turned to my father. 'And what about you, Eric? Wouldn't *you* like a little brother or sister for *your* birthday?'

My father thought about this. 'I'd rather have a cricket-ball, please,' he said.

One week something will not be as usual. As soon as I put my key in the door, I shall know something has changed. The lock will seem to yield more readily, the sitting-room curtains will be drawn wider to let in more light. On the front window-sill there will be a glass vase full of multicoloured dahlias.

This time he will not be standing at the sink, but sitting in his lounger by the patio doors, looking out at the garden. When I bend over to kiss him, his face will be smooth and quite dry. 'How are you?' I shall say, as usual.

'Oh. Not so bad.'

'I see you've got some flowers.'

'Oh. Yes.'

I wait for him to go on, but he just sits, smiling into the green outside.

'Where did they come from?'

He will say vaguely, 'Oh . . . I don't know. Someone brought them. Yesterday afternoon, I think it was.'

'A neighbour?' I shall prompt him. 'Carol? Rhona?'

'Someone like that.' He will smile again. 'I don't really remember.'

'They're pretty.'

'Yes,' he will say. 'She must have picked them from her own garden.'

*

43

One afternoon my father will look at me sideways. 'Are you coming over next Thursday?'

'I always come on Thursdays,' I tell him. 'Why?'

'Oh, nothing . . .' He rubs his hands on the knees of his trousers. 'It's just . . . Next Thursday . . . I'd like you to meet someone.'

I blink.

'It's someone I met at the lunch-club. Her name's Carolyn. I've been telling her all about you.'

Before I can turn my key in the lock my father's front door will swing open. A woman will be standing there on the threshold, smiling. She will be younger than my father, about sixty-five, with grey hair tinted to a blush, and lipstick. Her eyebrows have been plucked almost to nothing and redrawn in an arch that looks like surprise.

'Hello,' I'll say. 'You must be Carolyn.'

'Hello, Susan. I'm so happy to meet you! Do come in. Your father's just taking a nap. But the kettle's on. I thought we'd have tea on our knees, if that's OK by you.'

I feel like saying, 'Sure!' I find myself grinning at her. 'Are you American?'

She takes my jacket from me and arranges it on a hanger. She is smiling at my embarrassment. 'No. But I did live in the States for a while, until my second husband died. Then I decided it was time to come back home.'

'And you met my father at the lunch-club?' I can't believe it.

'Well . . .' She will touch me on the shoulder, in that way Americans have. 'I just go there to help out sometimes. I figured it was a good investment!' Under the eyebrows her eyes are shining. They are a soft, pale blue.

I shall follow her into the sitting-room, in a kind of daze. My father will look up from his chair. 'Darling!' he'll say to me. 'You've met Carolyn! She's been so kind to me. She made a cake!' And I shall hear something like triumph in his voice.

*

'Oh, shoot!' she will say, as the cake crumbles at the centre.

'It doesn't matter,' I say. 'It'll taste the same. I'm sure it's delicious.'

And it is delicious. It will be mouth-watering, an old-fashioned coconut cake, moist and surprising.

'It *is* delicious,' my father will tell me proudly. 'Carolyn's cakes are always magnificent.' And she will laugh, a crumb at the corner of her mouth, waving his compliments away.

'I thought you didn't like coconut?' I shall say to him.

My father keeps a snapshot of my mother on the dining-room table, next to his leather place-mat. It is a recent picture, taken in the garden of their friend's house in Wiltshire. My mother and father are in deckchairs, squinting into the sun. They are both smiling. My father looks relaxed. My mother looks tired.

When I go to see him my father always cries. For minutes he clings to me and sobs, without any words.

'I love you,' I keep telling him. 'You have to cheer up. You have to try.'

The crying stops. 'I do try,' he says, pathetically. 'You're everything to me. I think you're wonderful. You, and John, and Emily and Bridget. I don't know what I'd do without you. I've got a marvellous family.'

'You must *try* to cheer up,' I tell him again.

He smiles faintly. Then he picks up the photograph and looks at it. The strange noise starts up again.

One morning I shall turn the key in the lock and be greeted by silence. No high, thin wail will drift down to me from my father's bedroom, making me stop in my tracks in the hall to listen. There will be no sound from the kitchen. I shall put his pile of clean laundry down on the stairs and go into the dining-room.

And he will be lying there, across the rug with the roses on it, one hand still resting on the plastic arm of the chair he reached out for as he fell.

His face will be grey. I shall go up to him and touch him. He will be quite cold. He won't be breathing. I shall go back into the hall and lift the receiver. The pile of neatly pressed laundry will be next to my feet.

When I was sixteen, just old enough for X films, my father and I would go to the pictures together. What we liked best was horror.

Dracula, Son of Dracula, Return of the Living Dead, human skin bubbling up as if under acid, red titles consumed by flames or dripping blood. In the worst bits we would move closer together in the dark.

On the way home we would marvel. 'Did you recognize that churchyard? It was the same one they used in *Kiss of the Vampire*! Did you notice? Even the gravestones were the same!'

'And that shot of the tin-mine! It was the same one!'

Sometimes in the dark he would lean over to me and whisper, 'You see that man who's supposed to be the doctor?'

'What about him?'

'Don't you get the feeling you've seen him somewhere before?'

And as the carriage careered towards the silhouetted castle, the shafts of sunlight falling ever more obliquely across a familiar stretch of forest path, he would nudge me. I could just see him grinning in the dark.

At the seaside we used to go walking sometimes on the cliffs. I can remember clambering up steep dry paths to a sudden astonishment of wind and light over waves breaking. 'You go first,' my father would say to me. 'You can go on ahead, if you like.'

I would stand on my own at the top, the salt wind pulling tears from the corners of my eyes, and watch my parents come up the path towards me. My mother in a headscarf, the little tickly wisps of hair waving across her forehead. My father already walking in that characteristic way he had, stopping to look up at me, leaning slightly backwards. 'That's right,' he would say, when they finally caught up with me. 'You be the scout.'

'What does that make me?' my mother would ask him, laughing.

46

'You're the advance guard.' My father had his arm round her shoulders. 'And I'm the Main Body.'

When my parents called in to see me, my mother always arrived first. I would hear a knock at the front door and see her blurred shape through the stained glass. 'Eric's just parking the car.' She would come in and take off her mac. She would put her basket down on the kitchen table and pull out a piece of cardboard cut from the side of a cereal packet. On it something would be scribbled in blunt pencil. She would look at me, still pink and breathless. 'I've got so many things I want to tell you about. I had to make a list.'

One evening he will call me and I shall come at once. I shall walk into his sitting-room to find his television still on, the mauve and silver faces still flashing on the screen, lighting up the dark furniture. His chair will be empty.

I shall go upstairs to find him. He will be in the toilet, slumped against the wall, his trousers round his ankles. His face will be purple. I shall be able to make out the whites of his eyes, and his tongue.

He is too frail now to bath himself. Once a week he takes a shower, supporting himself against the tiled wall with one hand.

One day I shall come and bath him. I shall fill the bath with warm water and lean over it to test it with my elbow, as if it were for a baby. I shall help him undress.

He will get one leg over the side and for a long time we'll stand there in an odd kind of embrace. I shall feel him shaking. Then, slowly, he will manage to bring his other leg in next to the first and lower himself into the water.

I shall help him to wash himself. 'Would you like to soak for a bit?' I shall say. And I shall go downstairs to peel the vegetables. I shall turn on my mother's old radio so I can't hear him sloshing over my head. Then I shall hear something I recognize, a Chopin waltz or Mahler's Fifth. And I shall go out and get into the car and drive away.

My mother's bridge friends would always be ringing up, asking her for dates. She was probably the best and most sensitive player in the club. Sometimes she would ask me, half apologetically, 'You don't think Eric's really hard-done-by?' Then she would say, almost fiercely, 'I have to keep going. It's the one thing I do on my own. It would be so easy just to give in.'

Once a week my mother would go to the bridge club at Mayfield. On those evenings my parents would eat cold meat and baked potatoes. My mother would scrub and prick the potatoes before she left. It would be my father's job to put them in the oven at a time she would write down for him on a piece of cardboard.

We were descended from aristocrats, on my father's mother's side. She was a Butler, granddaughter of a younger son of the Earl of Ormonde. It was a family joke.

When one of us did something vulgar – licked jam off a knife, or picked our noses – we would remind one another of the Irish blue blood. 'Call yourself a Butler? No one would ever think you were descended from an Irish peer!'

His Lifeline button is upstairs on a window-sill. Or it is on the medicine cabinet next to his bed. 'Why don't you ever wear it?' I ask him. 'You're paying thirteen pounds a month, and you don't wear it.'

'I keep forgetting.'

'Do you wear it in the night?' I ask him. 'When you get up to go to the loo? I hope you do.'

'Oh, yes. I do when I remember.'

The next time I visit him the button is lying neatly rolled in its black neck-cord, on the shelf next to the phone.

*

I dream of the Death-bringer.

We burrow through a hedge and we are on a grassy slope crowded with people. There are parked cars with their boots open, people standing round with Thermos flasks and sandwiches, talking and laughing. There are sideshows. There is some kind of entertainment. I find myself thinking how lucky I am to have stumbled on all this.

And then it changes. I hear them whispering. I begin to understand: we are all only waiting. In a moment someone will move among us bringing death to anyone who meets his eyes. Several people will move among the crowd, but only one of them will be the Death-bringer.

I know what to do. I must keep moving myself. People will be frightened of me, they will think I am the one, but it is the only way to stay alive. I close my eyes and find I can see through my eyelids.

But then a group of men comes up behind me. I feel them rather than see them. One of them is speaking to me in a soft, insinuating voice. He has his hands gently on my waist. I am on the ground on my back and he is somehow still behind and above me. And he is telling me, cajoling me, mocking me to look at him. And I know he is the one. And I know that eventually I will.

In bed on weekend mornings my father would tell us his dreams. They weren't like our dreams. They all seemed to be long, intricate thrillers peppered with car-chases and bank robberies and guns. I could never work out how his dreams managed to be as exciting as a real detective story, while mine were only about evil spells and insects. The dreams my mother told were always about losing one of us. She had lost her little dog, Lindy, or her sister, Mona – or me – or my father.

About a month before my mother died she said to me, 'I've been thinking. I thought perhaps I'd try to write something about when we were girls. I keep remembering odd things. I thought I'd better start writing them down.'

'You should,' I told her.

'I just thought . . . when I can't sleep and I come downstairs in the middle of the night . . . I might as well be doing something.'

'I hope you're going to let me read it,' I said.

After her death I keep expecting to come across a wad of her close-written early memories.

For months nothing surfaces. It is as if she has left me a message that somehow I'm not equipped to receive. Then one day I am going through a pile of miscellaneous unused envelopes saved from greetings cards. She kept them inside the flattened Cellophane sheath from a bunch of flowers, folded over at the top and criss-crossed with rubber bands. As I sort the envelopes into sizes, a long thin slip of paper falls out, the kind of thing she used to write lists on. On it something is pencilled in her plain handwriting. 'Dad's housekeepers,' it says. 'Beattie.' Then:

Cousin Winnie. How scared we were.
Dad's oddments.
The time he came home from Maidstone market with the calf.
Hiding in the cabs with Mona to smoke, then eating raw onions
    to cover up the smell.
Bidge. Piano. Being so rude to her that time.
Jimmy Jenks.
William.

And then the one word in capitals: 'PEONI'.

I look at it. Is it a flower? Is it an acronym? My eyes come back again and again to that last word, as if by looking I could make it somehow fall open on everything she had wanted to say to me.

When I was very small I used to dream I had to pass through a wall of rock. I would go through it head first, through an impossibly small space. The rock would squeeze and squeeze my body from above and below until it was almost unbearable. My neck was always stretched, my head bent backwards. Then I would come out the other side, gasping. Even in the dream I always knew that in the end I would come out. It was as if I remembered.

I hear Emily singing along to her tapes, as she listens to them on her Walkman. You can't hear the tape; you can only hear her singing, like wailing. It reminds me of the odd, unearthly keening sound my father makes, to a tape we can't hear.

When I was a teenager he used to call my music a devil's tattoo.

My parents must have been among the first English couples to own a television. They bought it before I was born, a black and white nine-inch set that came alive at seven in the evening, when I was already in bed. My mother would watch it when my father was out playing. I must be among the few people of my age to have learned about the world from Andy Pandy and Bill and Ben.

During my adolescence our tastes seemed more or less to coincide. We all watched the news and the weather. We all watched sitcoms and serials and serious plays. We shared them. Afterwards we would discuss them. I watched *Quatermass* from the kitchen, through the crack in the door, because I was frightened to come any closer to the screen. And we listened to the radio too: Uncle Mac on a Saturday morning, *Family Favourites* and *Round the Horne* to the rising smell of Sunday joints. And *Journey into Space*. 'Go back! Do not come any further!' my father would say to me years later, in the sepulchral voice of an alien. We would all laugh.

Then our tastes diverged. The set always seemed to be flashing out some fantasy packed with American cops and shootings and car-chases. My mother would knit. I would spread my dress-patterns or patchwork pieces out on the floor to a background of gunshots, imploding flesh, crumpling metal. Sometimes she and I would go out and do chores together in the kitchen and talk.

Her programmes were always 'slow'. The films she loved were 'slow'. Her favourite was *Death in Venice*. My father would sit through her choices heroically. 'It was all right,' he would tell her afterwards. 'I didn't mind it. Nothing much seemed to happen, though. I kept wishing it would speed up a bit.'

Occasionally I would start to watch a serious discussion, or a programme about art or literature. After a few minutes my father would get up and leave the room. Then he would come back and poke his head through the door. 'What is this, Open University?' he would say.

Whenever there was a baby on television my father would call my mother in. 'Joy! *Joy!* Come and look at this! There's a baby!' And my mother would come in, still in her apron, and perch on the arm of a chair until the baby had gone.

I would watch too, trying to see what she saw in the plump flesh, the wrists with their bracelets of creases, the unfocused eyes, the drooling. 'What a sweet little thing!' my father would say. My mother would nod.

Sometimes she would protest mildly, 'It wasn't really crying. You could see it wasn't crying! It was just a recording of some other baby crying, somewhere else!'

My mother could never buy her bras off the peg in chain stores. She had to have them specially made. At regular intervals the Spirella lady would come and measure her. They would be together in the bedroom for half an hour. Then, a few weeks later, a new batch of long-line brassières would materialize, their elastic firm and smooth, their broad satin straps gleaming white or shell-pink.

Every morning my mother would sit on the bed to have her bra done up. Usually my father did it, but sometimes, when he was out or asleep, it was me. I would lean towards her warm back, grasp the two sides and yank until the rows of hooks and eyes almost met. 'Which one?' I would ask her.

'I don't know. The smallest?'

I would pull, and she would suck in. 'Are you sure?' I would ask her.

*

When I was in my teens and early twenties my father would hug my mother sometimes. He would look at me and say, 'You know Mum's got a lovely body. She's so cuddly! You know, I still get excited when I'm in bed and she's there, all warm, next to me. She's got such a lovely pair!'

My mother would look embarrassed. 'Oh, Eric, stop it!' she would say. Then, 'I hate them. I always have. They make me top-heavy. When I was at school I was so self-conscious . . .'

'They're lovely. I love them,' my father would say.

About a year after my mother dies I start to go through her dresses. The outer garments are all that is left of her clothes now. But there are so many of them. She has three whole wardrobes packed with the dresses, coats, suits and jackets she has been buying 'good as new' over the years. For several weeks I take whole armfuls of them home and wash them, to give to some charity. There are four dressing-gowns. Three winter coats. Five raincoats. Most of it seems to belong to some stranger. I find myself being especially meticulous as I iron the few things I ever saw her wear.

One of the dresses I remember is pure wool, and should never have been washed. It has shrunk two or three sizes. It is black. I put it on and look at myself in the mirror. It is flattering, though of another era. I take it off and fold it into the grey plastic rubbish-bag with the others.

One day he will be out when I get to his house. I shall see at once that the garage is empty, the up-and-over door flung back. I shall park in the Close and walk up his drive to the door.

I shall go upstairs. I shall take off all my clothes. I shall pick up my mother's old bra from where it still lies draped over the chair, and put it on.

The huge cups will jut out under my chin, full of nothing. When I poke them with my finger they will dimple and crumple into dents like car-metal. I shall catch sight of myself in the leaning mirror and draw in my breath.

I shall look for something to fill them, opening and shutting cupboards, climbing on chairs to ransack the high shelves, pushing aside jams and marmalade and chutneys. At the very back there will be a package of dried beans.

I shall hear him come back, the sound of his engine in the drive, the garage door sliding shut, his Chubb key turning in the lock, and then the Yale key, clicking the door open as it swings inwards over the carpet with a little hiss. I shall hear him take off his coat and cap and hang them on the pegs in the hall. I shall hear him shuffling through to the kitchen to stand at the sink, picking up plates and cutlery from the draining-board. And then the keening will start, a thin high wail that knots my stomach as I hear it rise and fill the whole house.

And I shall come down and stand in the kitchen, just behind him. 'Darling,' I shall say to him.

He will jump and turn round. 'What the . . . ?'

And I shall stand there in my mother's girdle and long-line brassière, grinning. I shall turn round for him slowly. And the beans will trickle out of me on to the tiled floor, with a patter like light rain.

Sometimes my father would tell us jokes.

'There was once a man who left his home in Dublin to come and seek his fortune in England. His next-door neighbour, a Mrs Dunn, came to see him off. "And while you're there," she said, "will you look up my son and tell him it's time he wrote me a letter?"

' "Where does he live?" the man asked.

' "London," the old woman told him. "WC2. Sure, that's where you're going."

' "I will indeed," the man said.

'As soon as he arrived in London he stopped a passer-by and asked him. "Where's WC?" he said.

' "It's over there, gov. Just down them steps."

'So the man went down the steps. He knocked on the second door.

' "What is it? What do you want?" a voice called out.

' "Are you Dunn?" the man asked.

'A stranger emerged, buttoning his trousers. "Yes, why?"

'The man looked at him indignantly. "Why don't you write to your poor old mother in Ireland?" '

The day Emily and Bridget and I have tickets for the ballet my father phones me. His voice sounds strange, slightly lower and thicker than usual, like a tape that is running down. 'Are you all right?' I ask him. He says he thinks he may be getting a cold.

'Well, take care of yourself,' I tell him. 'Keep warm. Go to bed early. Listen, I'll ring you in the morning to make sure you're OK.'

The ballet is supposed to be a big treat for Bridget's birthday. I tell myself the only thing that matters is that my daughters should enjoy it. The dancers flit about like exotic fish, and my father's face stares out at me. We are on the South Bank, in the Royal Festival Hall. In the first interval we go out and stand on the balcony to look at the Thames in the dusk, the lights just beginning to gleam out over the river. Emily and Bridget are eating ice-cream. 'It's very quiet,' Emily says.

I look down at the railway bridge. It's eerie. There isn't a single train on it, no movement. It's a ghost line. 'What's happened to the trains?' I ask.

Then I become aware of conversations around me. 'A bomb-scare,' someone is saying. 'They found a package. They don't know how long . . . All the mainline stations . . .'

We go back into the auditorium. I don't say anything to the girls. My face is turned towards the dancers on the stage. But I am not seeing anything. I can't hear anything. I'm sweating. I've never known such panic. My precious daughters. The dark city. And no money: I haven't had time to get cash and I had just enough for the ice-creams and a programme. Crazily my mind veers off and then fixes on practical details: what can I do about my contact lenses? How and when shall I ever get the chance to take them out?

I concentrate on not revealing any of my anxiety to the kids. They seem to enjoy the performance. When we come out, Bridget links her arm through mine. 'We'll go down to the information desk and see what we can find out,' I say.

But as we turn to go down, we look out over the river. It is quite dark now: the embankment lights ripple their pathways out over the water. And as we watch, a train pulls slowly out of Charing Cross and over the bridge towards us, its windows flick past us in a gold procession. We hear its low rumble change to something higher as it picks up speed.

The next morning the telephone wakes me at six. It is my father. 'Susan?'

'Yes?'

'I've been trying to get you.'

'Trying to get me?' I repeat blankly. 'When?'

'All yesterday evening. And you didn't answer.'

I take a deep breath. 'But you know I took the girls up to London yesterday evening, to the ballet,' I tell him. 'It was for Bridget's birthday. You knew that. You knew we were going.' There is a long silence. 'Are you all right?' I ask him.

His voice is slightly strange. He is crying. 'I don't know. I think I may be feeling a bit peculiar,' he tells me.

'I'll be over as soon as I can. Just let me sort the girls out, and I'll come over.' I have a sudden thought. 'Have you eaten anything?'

'I don't remember. I was going to have supper. Then I think I felt too tired to get it, so I just went to bed.'

'Have breakfast,' I tell him firmly. 'Get up when you're ready and try to have a good breakfast. I'll be with you as soon as I can.'

When I get to him he is sitting in front of the television as usual. The remains of his breakfast are still on the coffee-table in front of him.

I make him lunch and then tea. I wash up, listening to my mother's old kitchen radio while he dozes. I make his bed and gather up his wet handkerchiefs. I clean his bathroom while I am waiting for him to finish his tea. There is nothing obviously wrong with him. 'Do you think you'll be able to get to bed on your own?' I say.

'Oh, yes.'

I lean over and kiss him goodbye. 'I've got to go back and cook our evening meal now. I've left the girls on their own. But I'll ring you again in the morning to see how you're getting on.'

The next morning I ring him and there is no answer. I ring again. He might be in the toilet or out in the garage, getting a can of something from the old meat-safe. And sometimes he just can't get to the phone in time, before it stops ringing. I count the double tones: fifteen, twenty, twenty-five. Still nothing. I'll try again in half an hour.

But half an hour later there is still no answer. I ring my aunt, whose house is only a quarter of a mile away from his. 'Auntie Mo, I can't get through to my father. He's not answering. I wonder, could you possibly . . . ?'

A few minutes later she is on the phone to me again. 'Sue, he was on the floor. On the landing. He seemed to be half asleep. We managed to get him back into his bed. He looks more or less all right, but you can't really tell. He seems to have given himself a black eye.'

I think quickly. 'I'd better come over and see him. I may decide to stay there with him for a bit. It'll take me about an hour to pack up our stuff and get us over there.'

'Oh, Sue . . .'

My aunt's voice sounds so like my mother's. As I thank her for going round to check on him, my own voice shakes.

When I get to his house he is sitting up in bed. His eye is spectacular. I find myself imagining that it is the visible symptom of some nameless internal bleeding. 'Do you remember falling?' I ask him.

He shakes his head. 'I don't think I fell.'

57

'What were you doing on the floor, then? Didn't you trip on something?'

'I didn't fall,' he says again.

'Well, then, what happened? You were on the floor. What were you doing on the floor?'

'I was on my way to the lavatory. And I suppose I just sort of slipped down. Slowly. And then I couldn't get up.'

'Well, I wish you hadn't slipped down slowly!' I am grinning. 'I'm going to stay here with you for a day or two. Until you perk up a bit.'

His face brightens slightly; the eye begins to look almost comical. 'Do you mean Emily and Bridget are here?' he says.

'Yes. We're all here. All three of us.' I go downstairs and stand in his front room. The woods and farmland stretch away from me, as far as I can see, towards Tunbridge Wells. But something catches my eye, a small blur of red on top of the television. It is his Lifeline button, its black neck-cord dangling half across the screen.

One day I shall be looking in the larder for a can of beans. 'They're not in there,' my father will say. 'We don't keep them in there.'

'Where *do* you keep them?' I shall ask him.

He will look at me as if I am a half-wit. 'In the garage. In the meat-safe. With the evaporated milk and the sardines.'

I won't sigh. 'I'd better go out there and get them.'

But he won't let me. He will pick up the bunch of keys from the top of the twin-tub and fumble with the back door. Then I shall hear him shuffle off into the garden.

And I shall be left looking into the open pantry, at the old chipped enamel saucepans, the row of hot-water bottles upside down on their hooks, the extra spin-drier they kept for emergencies, an old handbag of mine full of clothes-pegs. And next to it a big white plastic carrier-bag, bulging. I shall reach into it.

When he comes back he will put the tin of beans down on the stained yellow counter. He will reach into the drawer for a tin-opener. He will grunt as he presses the metal tooth down into the lid. The steel butterfly will begin to turn shakily on its axis.

Then, from behind him, I shall raise my arms like a dancer and bring the plastic bag down smoothly over his head.

When I was very small, my father made a miniature aeroplane propeller. I don't know how he did it. He was no woodwork expert. Perhaps he got a friend of his to make it for him. But somehow one day he produced this little windmill with smooth, curved angled blades. He painted it in aeroplane colours – khaki and olive green with a flash of blue. And he fixed it to the bonnet of our car. As we drove along, it spun in the wind, a blur of motion, its circles superimposed on the road ahead, as if our car were about to take off.

'How was the club on Tuesday?'

He will look at me, smiling an odd kind of smile. 'Let me show you something.'

'What?'

'Come upstairs and I'll show you.'

I shall follow him upstairs as he pulls himself laboriously up by the banisters. I shall restrain myself from pushing. He will open the door of the back bedroom and wave his hand with something that seems like pride. 'There.'

'What?' He is blocking the doorway and I can't see anything. I shall wait for him to move.

'There!' he will say again.

I'll blink. On top of the double bed there will be a small pile of miscellaneous objects: chocolates, toiletries, embroidered handkerchiefs, notelets, a woman's mock sealskin purse, a bottle of low-alcohol wine. 'What is it? Where has it come from?'

'I won it in the raffle.'

'What, all of it?'

'Yes.'

'But you must win a prize every week!' I shall look at him doubtfully.

'I do,' he will say. 'More or less.'

I shan't know what to say. I shall almost tell him he must have green fingers. 'Well,' I'll say in the end, 'perhaps you should take up gambling on a larger scale.'

As I drive away, I shall still be able to see it, his little mound of goodies, the double bed under them, the pink candlewick bedspread dented with their weight. I shall wonder if I'll live to regret my remark about gambling. Then I visualize his figure like a bent maypole in the blowing ribbons of a betting-shop doorway.

And somehow the spool of string has worked itself loose from his hands, or from mine. I shall watch it jump and spin away from us over the cliff-top, catching and tearing at the clumps of sea-pinks and wind-blown, wiry grass. Already the distant smiling face will have begun to wobble, the string will have started to sag towards the waves.

Shall I be screaming? I'm not sure. All I see is the heavy stick bounding away, and my father's back as he runs to try to catch it before it reaches the edge. Then, even before he can get to it, the kite will steady on its string, the sag will suddenly seem less noticeable.

'What's happened?' I shall look up at the sky, and from the sky to his face.

But he will be as mystified as I am. I shall catch him up and together we shall walk carefully towards the edge. He will hold my hand to stop me from going too close. We'll stand side by side and look over. And there will be the spool, almost bare now, wedged firmly in the multiple trunks of a bush that will seem to grow straight out of the cliff-face. I shall squat beside him as he lies on his stomach on the grass and reaches over. Holding the stick firmly with one hand, he will prise the spiky branches apart. Then, clutching the stick to his chest, he will clamber awkwardly to his feet. Together we shall inch backwards the way we have come, the small square face rising higher and higher. After a while we shall turn and begin to walk normally, the string cutting

60

across his shoulder. As we walk towards the car, the kite will still be rising over the sea behind us.

She would write lists on bits of cardboard cut from cereal packets. She would save plastic bags and wash them. She would turn them inside out and hang them up to dry on the line. For a year after her death a single small white polythene bag flaps in all weathers. By spring it is in shreds. In July I finally unpeg it and throw it away.

When my father first went to the grammar school, the family was too poor to buy him a school cap.

When he was in the sixth form, he was the only boy still in short trousers. He never had a suit.

And then my grandmother bought him a suit. It was purple.

I realize almost immediately that it isn't any use. My father stands at the gate to catch his breath, his two small feet side by side on the sunlit gravel, the aluminium of his tripod gleaming. A young woman comes towards us with a dog on a lead. 'Can I help you?'

'We've come to see Mrs Sanderson at 2.30,' I tell her. 'We're a bit early.'

'Let me open the door for you. That'll make life easier.'

She covers the ten paces of path in a moment and comes back, then swings easily out of the gate and turns downhill, the dog pulling on its lead. At my shoulder, my father inches forwards, towards the door she has opened for him.

We are too early. An elderly lady introduces us into the dining-room. I see her glance at the tripod. My father shuffles past her and lowers himself with a sigh on to a straight-backed chair. I sit facing him across an African violet in a pot.

The table is already laid for supper: six mats, six place-mats, six napkins in assorted holders. I stand up and walk past them to the bay window. On the other side of the glass it is all sunlight and green dapple, flowers in borders, a terrace with white garden furniture and a printed parasol, a lawn sloping away towards high hedges. Deserted. 'Nice garden,' I say to him.

He nods. I want to say, 'Come and look.' I want to pick him up and carry him to where he can see it. But for him to cross the few feet of carpet will take at least fifteen minutes. Someone might come in when he is halfway across, and then he will have to turn round and come all the way back.

The women who interview us, two rather glossy, well-dressed females in their late fifties, are pleasant enough, though they frown slightly when I tell them we have not completed the financial statement. 'I'm afraid you do have to complete it,' one of them explains to us. 'If you should decide to take the room.' She looks at him, then at me. I look away. I think she doesn't know which one of us to address her remarks to. I find myself wishing she would make up her mind.

'Well, let's go and have a look at the room, then, shall we?' she says brightly. Already the door, the glimpsed hall, the newel-post of the worn old staircase, are beginning to recede. But my father makes an effort. I can see he is trying hard to put on a good show. At the foot of the stairs I take the tripod from him, and he goes up, the woman called Mrs Sanderson leading the way. I follow just behind him. He goes up less slowly than usual, using both hands to hoist the dead weight of his body from step to step. Near the top there is a small square landing, where a short flight continues at right angles. 'Nearly there,' someone says. Then, just at the top, the twin balustrades end and he is left hanging backwards, his feet already on the last step, his hands at the ends of the rails. Mrs Sanderson turns and watches him, uncertain whether to offer her arm. For a moment he dangles there just above me like a great insect. Then, almost imperceptibly, he seems to regain control, the weight somehow invisibly transferred, the fall averted. 'I think it's clear that this staircase is going to be too much for you,' Mrs Sanderson says.

*

62

The room itself is small and empty, the curtainless window white with sun. There is only a battered locker with an electric hot-plate, and a newish patterned carpet. We stand there a moment in silence.

Then someone says encouragingly, 'I expect your wife gave you a lot of support when she was alive.'

'She did. She was marvellous.' I hear the catch in his voice, but he is standing against the light, and I can't see any tears.

I say, 'But you supported her too. You gave her what she needed. You were a good team.' I look round for Mrs Sanderson. 'It's hard, when you've been together for fifty years . . .'

But he is already telling them about his falls, his giddiness, his meals on wheels. 'I still drive, you know,' he tells them. 'I go shopping in the village. I cook my own dinners.' They assure him he is wonderful. But they can see the despair written all over us. 'And you,' someone says, looking at me, 'it sounds as if your life is rather hectic.'

I nod. Suddenly I can't speak. Suddenly their faces against the bare walls are dissolving. Through the white sunlight I can just recognize the garden, the same tall trees.

The pictures on the stairs are a blur now too, and the geometrically patterned stained glass above them. This time my father chooses a more comfortable chair. They smile and dismiss us gently, giving me a contact name and phone number, mentioning alternatives. I scarcely hear them. It keeps rising in me like nausea and I am frightened I will cough it out and it will disgrace me. I ask them if they will be kind enough to write the name down.

At the end they offer to walk my father to the front gate while I go for the car. I hardly wait even to thank them. As I walk back to my parking spot I take great gulps of the summer afternoon. Halfway along the road I see a man in his forties open the door of a blue Escort and throw a briefcase on to the back seat. A young woman comes towards me with a child in a pushchair and as they pass me the toddler leans out and pulls a leaf from the hedge. Privet. When I turn the ignition key, it slips between my fingers, and I realize that for some time I have been crying.

I dream I go to a café to meet someone. And when I get there, I discover the person I am meeting is my mother. I walk in and look round the room, and there she is, sitting alone at a table, waiting for me. In front of her there are tea-things, a stainless steel teapot, a jug of hot water, a bowl of sugar, a smaller jug of milk. I go over to where she is. I sit down next to her. She picks up the teapot and begins to pour. And I find myself watching her every gesture, the way she lifts her arm, the angle of her elbow as she bends it, the shape her fingers make on the handle. And I am marvelling. I keep looking and looking at her. I touch her to make sure she is warm and real. And the tears are streaming down both our faces. And I realize it is exactly the same for her as it is for me.

My mother was always too hot. From menopause onwards, she always seemed to be flushed and agitated. She would open a window in the sitting-room. She would open the kitchen door to let out the steam.

She would be in the kitchen, her face rosy as she cooked or washed up, in a light summer dress. My father would sit in front of the television, his feet on the hearth, the gas fire burning.

When I told my parents I was going to have another baby, my mother's faced dropped. 'Oh, *darling* . . . Are you *sure*?' She tried to reason with me. She told me what a lot of work babies were.

Once my mother lost her temper. It was just after Bridget was born. We were at my parents' house. I was kneeling on the floor to change Bridget's nappy, and Emily came up behind me, screaming and hitting me on my back and shoulders. And my mother ran over and scooped her up and smacked her. 'You mustn't hit Mummy like that!' She was shaking with anger.

*

64

My mother would sit on the beach at Cooden, in the shelter of a breakwater, knitting socks while we played. Every other year she would make them from scratch, the grey wool looped over one finger as it flew across the stitches. And the next year she would unravel the feet and reknit them, one size larger.

She made my green check school dresses. She decorated them with ricrac. She knitted my green cardigans. She adjusted the straps on my grey pleated skirts.

At every moment someone somewhere is drawing a curtain. Someone is dying. Someone is learning to write in joined-up writing. Someone is picking up a grain of rice with chopsticks. Someone is forcing a needle through leather with a thimble. Someone is bursting a balloon and crying. Someone is reaching down into damp earth. Someone is extracting a tooth. Someone is playing chess. Someone is finding a bag of cotton-reels in an attic, dreaming of insects, choking on a fishbone, sharpening a pencil. Someone somewhere is dancing to unsuitable music.

When people asked me which of my parents I preferred, I always said my father.

In my mother's book, the worst sin was lying. Nothing else ever mattered.
   She had been lied to, I suspected, as a child, quite often.

One day I shall put on my mother's black dress. It will have shrunk to about three inches above my knees. I shall put on sheer tights and black shoes, a silk scarf to hide the dated neckline. I shall wear my beige linen jacket over it, the one with the shoulder-pads. I shall catch the next train to London.
   And as I get off the train I shall see one particular face float up from the crowd, watching me. Clear brown Spanish skin, good American teeth, dark eyes, mouth slightly twisted in that irony I

seem to remember. And I'll look away. And then I'll feel a hand resting lightly on my shoulder. And I'll look up.

Once I wake up at night galvanized with anxiety, and nothing I can do will make it go away. I lie staring into the darkness, listening to John's breathing, trying to match my own to his rhythm. The darkness is full of patterns, swarming red and orange. In the end I get up and go downstairs to the first floor.

I tiptoe into the little back room where Bridget is curled up in the bottom bunk. I climb carefully into the top bunk without waking her. I lie there until I can make out the shape of the window, its pale rectangle of morning. Then I sit up quietly. I lower myself down the ladder, rung by rung. I slide my body in between her warm covers. And she turns sleepily and puts her arms round me, as if she expected to find me there. And we sleep.

The kite he had made me was as beautiful as anything I had ever imagined.

It was constructed in the usual way, a split cane notched and bound in position at the centre, an outer web of fine, tough string, a huge square of brown paper, folded and pasted with geometrical precision. An extra circle to reinforce it in the middle. A long tail weighted with bows of neatly folded newspaper. The same simple, flawless design that brought kids running from every corner of the beach or field wherever we found ourselves. But this time he had perfected it. This time it had a glittering tail covered in foil and brightly painted features that would smile at me from the sky.

Together we laid it out on the cliff-top, the long string reaching back towards him in the direction of the wind, and the tail beside it, undulating across tufts of waving grass. I lifted it up by its crossed cane skeleton and felt the wind push it back against my body. I watched the gusts ripple towards me across the cliff. He lifted the string at his end until the slack hung free between us. I felt a gust almost wrench the cane cross from my grasp and he shouted, 'Now!'

66

I let go and it rose straight from my hand. The huge tail lifted steadily bow by bow, peeling off like a strip of skin, until it swung out over the sea, catching new currents and swaying with a kind of life. I ran back towards him across the headland, still looking up into the sky, almost tripping on a clump of grass. 'Oh, *yes!*' I shouted. '*Yes!*'

'Would you like to hold it?' He held out the big gnarled stick the string was wound on.

I looked up at the distant smiling square of paper that still bobbed and swam in summer cloud, scarcely bigger now than a stamp. I nodded.

And then something happened. Before I could grasp it properly, the stick was spinning and jumping away from me, catching at the wiry grass and tearing, then scraping the face of the cliff in a shower of little pebbles. I watched it bounce towards the edge, as the line went heavy and the kite hung wobbling. Then the distant smiling face tipped towards me and the end of the tail brushed the surface of the sea. I saw it fall and float for a moment, slipping sideways between the waves. I watched the brown paper go darker and darker until finally I lost it against the water.

The day we take him to Greenfield House he is in a kind of daze. It is the first week of Wimbledon, and the television is on. Sun streams into his front room. We draw the curtain across to lift him from his chair and take off his pyjamas. We dress him. I push his feet into his shoes like a child's and tie the laces. He uses the commode in the kitchen.

It takes us about half an hour to get him across the threshold. He is keening quietly, in that way he has. At the threshold itself he bends down with infinite slowness. He starts to pick up bits from the hall carpet – a blade of dried grass, a bruised honey-suckle-trumpet. But it isn't those he wants. He points to something he can't quite reach. 'This?' I say. 'This?' But he wails, shaking his head. His lower lip wobbles. I follow his pointing finger. Then he nods, appeased. I pick up the offending chip of black gravel and put it carefully in his hand.

Part Two

I DRIVE ROUND the block, turn back towards the town, down London Road beside the Common. Then I double back up to the station roundabout and up Grove Hill Road, dodging cars. Up the private road, through the heavy gates, coming almost to a complete stop at each sleeping policeman. Down that hill with the field of sheep, with its verges of brambles and bracken. I turn into the drive, my father's little car bouncing gently into and out of the familiar potholes. I come to a halt on that terrace above the wide lawn that must once have been a tennis court. I see the circular white table with its ring of chairs, the residents and relatives nodding vaguely in welcome under the parasol. The thick creeper twines up and up under my father's window.

He is inside, his back towards the open door. I kiss him before he has time to see me. He looks up, his eyes full of tears. 'What a lovely surprise!' he says.

It is always a surprise, for both of us. Each week he knows I am coming. I always tell him when to expect me. Yet every week he is as surprised as if it were the first time.

Every year on my mother's birthday my father gave her a card. The same card. A photograph of red roses in a basket with 'To My Darling Wife' on it in embossed silver lettering, and a red ribbon bow in the corner. Inside, a rhyme, and 'Eric' in his neat handwriting. He had written just 'Joy' on the envelope. He never sealed it. On the morning of her birthday he would slip it in among the others.

After a few days she would give it back to him, and he would put it away, for the next year. Then it would appear again, the red roses only slightly out of date, the red ribbon only very slightly faded.

When she let me look at her cards she always asked, 'Did you see Eric's?' in a special voice, half affectionate and half amused. But she always stood it in the place of honour in the centre, next to the clock.

*

71

'Do you realize it's your birthday next week?' I shall ask him, one afternoon when I am visiting.

He will look almost interested. 'Is it really?'

'Yes. Had you forgotten? Look, give me your little diary and I'll write it in for you. Then you won't forget.'

He nods. He is quiet for a moment while I write it. Then he says, 'How old am I going to be?'

'Eighty-two,' I tell him. 'You know that. Come on.' Then I shall say carefully, 'We thought you might like to come out for a meal with us to celebrate, like last year.'

He will consider. Then he'll say, 'Or perhaps you could all come here. Perhaps we could have a party here, one evening?'

He will be sitting in his room, in the single chair, holding court. John and the girls will sit on his bed. I'll be perched on the edge of the commode.

In the doorway Sister Latham will raise her glass. 'To Eric!' she will say. 'Eighty-two today! Many happy returns!' The sherry will glint in our glasses.

Then he will turn to me and say, 'Do you know, if Joy . . .' His voice will catch slightly, but he will go on. 'If Joy could see me now, I think she'd say . . . I'm doing . . . all right.' He will gulp at his sherry and smile across at us, his eyes full of tears.

I dream of the perfect meeting, the moment of recognition you have only in dreams. I meet someone, and I look at them, and they look back at me. And they *know*. Sometimes I think I would do anything, drive anywhere, to preserve that simple knowledge.

My parents would joke sometimes about death. Every few years my father would change his car for a new one 'to see me out'.

My parents would joke sometimes about death. They rarely spent money on themselves. But occasionally one of them would splash out. They would show me their new pairs of summer shoes.

72

'These should see us out,' they'd say. They would look at each other and laugh.

My father's clothes are draped over the back of a chair, waiting to be marked with his name. They are like dead grasses, leaves, their colours are the colours of hips and haws, woody nightshade. His brown tweed jacket reminds me of the brown of winter fields. It is like labelling specimens for a nature table – 'Eric Wicks', 'Eric Wicks', 'Eric Wicks'.

He was always short. Five foot three in his stocking feet. When he passed out top of his group in the final RAF navigational exams, he would normally have been made an officer. But they told him explicitly that he was too small. The men would never respect him. He became a warrant officer. His mates nicknamed him Lofty. 'Lofty's binding away like hell,' one of them had written on a postcard to my mother.

When I was a child he would tell me this story. 'Too benign,' he would say, laughing. 'What a funny shape!'

Sometimes I would prolong the agony of my homework late into the evening. Sometimes, if I didn't understand something immediately, I would get upset and refuse to understand it at all. He would come home at seven to find me crying.

Once it was geometry, a scale drawing I had already laboured over, the lines on the page of my book all messy and blurred with tears. 'It doesn't work,' I told him. 'It's supposed to meet, but it won't come out right.'

And he must have put his arm round me. 'Look,' he said. 'We'll do it as it really is, as it's meant to be.'

And he got a fresh pencil and a long metal ruler and drew it on the wall – not to scale, but life-size, great triangles that would loom over our kitchen table for months afterwards like painted gods.

One afternoon I drive him to the optician's. On the gravelled forecourt I stop the car and unload the Zimmer. I open his door and lean over him to help him with the clasp of his seat-belt. He struggles to swing his legs sideways and out over the sill to meet the path. I end up lifting his right foot in my hands to help him. Then, holding him firmly under his left arm as I have seen the nurses do, I help him up. For a moment he stands there swaying, and I think his legs are going to buckle under him. But no. 'Lean forward,' I tell him, and bit by bit we manage to cross the few yards of space to the optician's front door. I look back at our exotic footprints, swirled behind us like the prints of some mythical beast.

I have allowed fifteen minutes for those ten yards, but still we manage to be late. Already the receptionist is watching our progress with a kind of disbelief.

'Just a few more inches and I'll be able to close the door behind you,' I say.

He looks up and sees the receptionist among her green plants. He smiles at her sweetly. 'I wonder if you have a Gents I could use?'

When we get back to Greenfield House, Sister Latham is there to help us. She is laughing as she brings the wheelchair, sun in her eyes, welcoming him home. His face brightens. I watch as she manoeuvres him skilfully out and up the ramp. I hold the doors open and then close and bolt them behind him.

As we cross the hall, Vera wanders past us, hands clasped in front of her, wide eyes fixed on some distant high object, muttering to herself. She stops at my side and gently touches my elbow, links her arm through mine, patting and stroking my hair with her other hand. The haunted eyes stare at me, as I catch whispered fragments: 'I see you . . . came here . . . lovely . . . you're lovely, you are . . . lovely.'

Sister Latham breaks in, laughing softly, detaching the confiding fingers from my jacket. 'Now, Vera. We're just bringing Eric in and getting him back into the lounge. It's all right.'

And Vera wanders away like a sleepwalker, her fingers still combing the air in front of her. 'You are. You're lovely.'

'Don't mind her.' Sister Latham's eyes crinkle in sympathy as we help my father off with his coat. But the hall with its faded curtains, its oil-paintings of heavy roses, the low bookshelf with his *Daily Mail* still on it unopened, everything begins to waver, flowing to earth slowly like old glass.

The small cactus on my window-sill was my mother's. It has survived a whole year of fierce sunlight without a single drink. The worms of growth were all shrivelled and irregular, with narrow, discoloured waists. Now I have chopped them all off and started to give it water. Now the old growth is almost invisible under a carpet of babies.

One of the residents of Greenfield House is a hamster. They keep him in a complicated structure of blue-tinted plastic set up in the sunny bay window. At the bottom is a globe where he can take exercise, running and running as the blue curve turns on its axis, never getting anywhere. He runs lightly, stopping occasionally to sniff the air. Then he starts again and the globe turns with his weight, keeping him motionless like an athlete on an exercise machine, keeping him hanging over the same blurred blue horizon.

More often he is asleep, curled invisibly into the nest of wood-shavings at the top of the plastic tower. Around him his fellow-residents doze, twitching, snoring intermittently. Once I saw a blue-uniformed auxiliary lean to top up his water-bottle as he slept.

The staff say he tends to be nocturnal: while the old people are upstairs in their beds he creeps out to sniff the darkness, plays with his toys and retreats again into the nest. The nurses are trying to teach him to wake up in the daytime, and sleep while the others sleep.

But he resists. I have hardly ever seen him playing. And even when he does, they stare at him blankly, as if the plastic tower were quite empty. I would have to be visiting this place at night, summoned by some emergency to my father's bedside, to be able to watch the sensitive whiskers emerge of their own accord, the little paws scrabbling at the plastic to get out.

For about five years his only topic of conversation was his eyes.

'Hello. How are you?' I would ask them both, as I hugged them, one after the other.

He never gave my mother time to answer. 'I'm having a bit of trouble with my . . .' he would begin.

Then I stopped asking. I would try to talk to my mother, or talk about anything else – the news, the TV, the weather. And whatever the topic, he would steer the conversation back to the same subject.

'No sign of this hosepipe ban ending,' I would say to him.

And he would screw up one eye. 'You see, when I look at you now, all I can make out is your shirt and your hair and your mouth moving. The rest is a blur.'

And I wouldn't know how to answer. 'Shall I make us a cup of coffee?' I would say.

Once, a few weeks before she died, I managed to tell my mother how I felt. 'I can't bear it,' I said. 'All those years with his eyes, and now they've done his eyes, it's something else. Now it's his knees. Everything's his knees. How do you stand it?'

'Poor Eric,' she said. 'He has so much to put up with. I often think I should be more sympathetic . . .'

My father was upstairs resting. We went into the dining-room and shut the door. The piano was open, the girls' music strewn across it. She rummaged in the piano-stool for something a bit more interesting and started to play tentatively from sight, laughing at her own mistakes. Her face had a kind of sweetness. 'Why did you get rid of our piano, when I stopped playing?' I asked her. 'It wasn't me who played well, it was you. Why didn't you hang on to it for yourself?'

Her laugh sounded rueful. 'I suppose I was cross with you for refusing to go on learning. I wanted to get rid of it. I wanted to be done with it all.'

'But now,' I said. 'Now you could . . .'

'Oh, now . . . Music. That was always Eric's thing.'

'But all that Chopin you used to play?' I objected. 'How can you let yourself believe that?'

'Oh . . .' She seemed to go into a dream. Her fingers were still moving faintly over the keys. Then she said, 'I've been thinking lately, that if . . . if Eric . . . if something were to happen . . . I might get . . . an electric organ.'

'An organ? A keyboard, you mean?'

'It wouldn't take up all that much room.'

'*Joy?*' My father was calling her from upstairs. I went out and stood in the hall to shout back. I filled my lungs with air and bellowed, 'She's down here, in the dining-room. Did you want something?'

Before she got the fostering job with Dr Barnardo's my mother used to cycle over to Four Elms to look after a family of children in the afternoons. She had a child's seat on the back of her bike. Occasionally she would ask permission to take me with her. More often she would leave me behind.

But one afternoon I was in a temper. I didn't want to let her go. I slipped away from my babysitter and got my dolls' pram out of the garage. Then I walked the three miles to where she was.

I can remember standing on the other side of a thick hedge, hearing other children's laughter, my mother's own calm, gentle speech-rhythms, through the tight leaves. Then Katriona caught sight of me. 'Susan Wicks is at the gate,' she said loudly.

'You mustn't tell stories, Katie,' I heard my mother say.

'But she *is*. I saw her. Susan Wicks *is* at the gate.'

'Don't be silly. She can't possibly be. She's at home, in Edenbridge. You mustn't tell fibs, darling.'

'She *is*!' Katriona's voice had risen to a squeak.

Then my mother sighed and came to the gate. She stood in the gap. The other children were jumping up and down, clinging to her hands. They were squealing. My mother looked at me. She looked at the dolls' pram, at my dolls, their greyish bedding shaken into a heap by the rough surface of the lanes.

My father can't seem to grasp the relationship between the care he receives in the nursing-home and money. Several times already he has asked me how much it costs to keep him here, and I have answered, but he doesn't remember. My answers get shorter.

'Fourteen thirty,' I tell him.

'A month?'

'A month.'

He is quiet for a bit, seeming to consider. Then he says, with a sort of wonder in his voice, 'That doesn't seem very much.'

I clarify. 'One thousand four hundred and thirty.'

He doesn't seem to hear me. Then at last he says, 'Oh.'

My mother did the chores. My father paid the bills. Sometimes now he looks at me and says, 'You know, there's one thing that makes me feel thankful.'

'What's that?' I ask him.

'Well . . . If I'd died first and Joy had been left on her own, she wouldn't have known what to do about all the money side of things. Poor darling. I don't know how she would have coped.'

My mother would sometimes write a cheque for my birthday. They had a joint account. But she never trusted herself. She would pass the cheque over to my father, to make sure she hadn't filled it in wrong.

When I slit open his bank statement and hand it to him in its envelope, he fumbles with the folded paper as if it were something fragile. He sits reading it for about ten minutes. 'Is the balance healthy?' I ask him.

'Yes. It looks like it. Five hundred pounds.'

'Good,' I say. Then, 'You know it doesn't mean much. You understand what I'm doing, that every month I'm transferring just enough to cover what you need.'

There is a long pause. Then he says, 'I can see where they took the £1,430 for this place.'

'It's a standing order. It goes through automatically.'

He considers. 'I suppose that's not too bad when you think that it's for several months.'

'No,' I correct him. 'It's for one month. That's what it costs.'

He folds up the statement carefully and pushes it back into the torn envelope. 'It seems a lot of money.'

'It is,' I say. 'But that's what it costs. That's what they all cost, more or less.'

He takes up the bunch of leaflets that came with his electricity bill and starts to read them: electric shower, customer charter, remote-control hearing-aid, he reads them all minutely one by one. For about half an hour I sit by him in silence as the glossy leaflets float down one by one into his lap.

My father would say, quite often, 'If anything ever happened to Joy, it'd be the end of me. I'd be finished.'

It is the same now every Sunday: the three of us in his small car, as I drive him back through the dusk. In my mirror I can see John trapped behind the Zimmer-frame, as if he is behind bars. My father is in the front beside me, telling me again how short it seems, this journey back to Greenfield House. In a matter of minutes we draw up on the terrace, where the yellow light is streaming from bay windows. Every week, on Classic FM, they seem to play the same tunes. Tonight it is 'Nimrod' from the 'Enigma' Variations. Who are we and where are we going? I ask myself. How will we know when we have arrived?

When my mother started a new job on a maternity ward, she bought herself a car, a Fiat 500. She would drive back from the local hospital after a late shift, through dark, overgrown lanes. You could hear her coming for miles, the characteristic chug of her engine announcing her arrival through silence.

*

Driving my father backwards and forwards now between here and Greenfield House, I am real and yet somehow outside myself, as if I existed only to music. Today it is the Third Brandenburg Concerto. It seems like a part of us, of this moment, of the windswept late-summer streets. Our lives are a film that is all opening titles and end-titles, with nothing in between.

I try to see the world through my father's eyes. I sit here and make myself as small and still as I can, and the trees seem to fade from my window. Knuckles of wisteria tap on the glass. In the nursing-home wardrobe, my old clothes seem to belong to another body.

It was my father who told me most of what I learned about sex. My mother would look into space and mutter something vague about love and 'a nice warm feeling'. But my questions called for something more specific. When I came home hot from a train-carriage of girl-talk, I would demand of her, 'Mum, what's a wet dream? What's fellatio? How do you do contraception?'

And she would say, 'Daddy knows more about all that than I do. Wait till he gets home and ask him. He'll tell you about it all.'

And when he had finished telling me, she would sometimes say, to our great amusement, 'He's wonderful. He's a mine of information. He taught me everything I know about intercourse.'

'?'

'You won't believe this. But I never even knew what a homosexual was until I married your father.'

One afternoon at Greenfield House my father says to me, 'I had a funny feeling this morning when I woke up.'

'What kind of funny feeling?' I ask him.

'Oh, I don't know . . .'

'You mean you felt dizzy? More than usual?'

'No. No. Not dizzy. More a sort of feeling I had.'

On the television in front of us a young, virile-looking

Australian is lying half propped up in bed. *Doctor, you're hiding something. What is it?* 'What kind of feeling?' I say again.

He says in a small, quiet voice, 'I had the feeling I was going to die today.'

'Well, you haven't managed it so far,' I tell him.

He is silent for a moment. Then he says again, 'I woke up, and I just had this funny feeling I was going to die.'

I don't know what to say to him. *You can't die. I can't imagine life without you.* I lean over and kiss him. For half an hour I don't let go of his hand.

One night he will call me. 'Susan? Is that you?' he will say. His voice will be slurred and strange.

'Where are you ringing from?' I shall ask him.

'Greenfield House. I asked forth' phone, and they let me have it. I told them I needed ttalk to you.'

It sounds unlikely. 'Are you all right?' I shall ask him.

'No's' bad. But I wouldn' mind . . .'

'What?'

Silence. Then, 'Can you leave Emily and Bridgt?'

'I'll be over to tuck you up in about ten minutes,' I shall say.

When I get there I shall run straight up to his room, without saying anything to the nurses. I shall look at him closely.

But he'll wink at me and lean over, fishing for something between the bed and the wall. He'll pull up a wine-glass. Then he'll fish again and pull up another one. He'll put them down carefully in a hollow of the quilt, side by side. Then he'll lean down again and pull up a bottle of sherry. It will be two-thirds empty. 'You forgo' ttake it with you,' he'll say to me. 'Will you have one?'

'Why not?' I grin. 'What's the toast?'

'Thfuture,' he says. He raises his glass.

I raise my own glass and touch it to his. 'Thfuture,' I say.

When I am with him now I feel like a virtuoso. I slit his envelopes with amazing dexterity. I can slip through a door in seconds, run upstairs to put away his things, and be back before he has even noticed I am gone. I can balance my tea-cup on my knee without spilling a drop. I can jump into the car and turn the key in the ignition and drive away.

More and more now I dream that my mother is alive.

In the dreams she is perfectly herself, perfectly ordinary. She is talking and smiling. I wonder if she is getting too tired.

Then I wake up. All day I carry the dream of her round with me, a kind of sweetness.

It is late May, the anniversary of my mother's death, but my father will no longer remember. I shall choose this day to take him out.

I shall drive him into the country, to somewhere beautiful – Scotney or Sissinghurst. I shall get him into his wheelchair and push him slowly between banks of azaleas and rhododendrons. In the gaps, the green slopes will ripple away from us. We'll sit at a small table in the afternoon sun and have a cream tea.

He takes a long time to eat it. He chews each mouthful slowly and then washes it down with tea. The china cup shakes in his hand. There is a circumflex of cream on his moustache.

I lean back in my chair and squint up at the sun through branches. The discs of light overlap and fuse. Around me there are voices, insects, the clink of his spoon on the saucer. I close my eyes.

He touches me on the shoulder. I open my eyes. 'Look,' he says. 'Did you see that?'

'What?' For a moment I can't see anything.

And he will point to a rhododendron flower almost at his elbow, a huge pink pearl, almost too heavy for the stalk.

'What?' I shall say again.

'There. In that flower. Look.'

And as I watch an enormous bee will crawl out of one of the flower-trumpets. For a moment it will rest on the pink lip, its fur ruffling slightly in the breeze. Then the fat body will lift slowly and blunder away.

When people asked me which of my parents I preferred, I always said my father.

My father is going to the hospital for an assessment. What will they make of him? I wonder. Will he fail? Will he pass with flying colours?

He will have refused to have the cataract operations. By the time my mother dies he will see everything through a dense fog. At her funeral I shall take his arm and lead him into the front pew. He will close one eye and squint at the coffin on its platform, with its mound of flowers. He will lean over and say to me, 'You see, when I look at her now, all I can see is a sort of smudge.'
    'What colour smudge?' I shall ask him.

My father was always interrupting my mother. She would start hesitantly to explain the delicate dynamics of her bridge circle, and my father would cut her off with a detailed narrative of the plot of some TV series.
    By the time she died she had fallen into the habit of not finishing her sentences.

On winter evenings my father would roast chestnuts at the open fire. He bent an old shovel so it would rest against the grate, and pierced it with holes. He called it his Chestnut-Roaster Mark One. When the chestnuts burned and yet were still raw, he modified it slightly. It became the Chestnut-Roaster Mark Two. The contraption got more and more complicated. I think it was the Mark Five that was finally successful. The pierced metal let the glow from the coals shine through like orange stars.

He hit me only once, in the kitchen. I can't remember what I had done. He smacked me once on the hand, 'a little *tap* that wouldn't have hurt an *insect*!' And my reaction took them both completely by surprise. When I was forty, he would still remind me of it and laugh.

There is a strip of sun across my kitchen floor, broken by the uprights of the window-frame. It is like the dotted line along the middle of the road, but luminous, a holy road going through my kitchen. I could try to follow it. I could try to place my feet perfectly without stumbling or collapsing. The brick-red quarry tiles are turning yellow.

The warmest room in our old house was always the kitchen, with its old Aga in the corner, its quarry-tiled floor, its little red spiders crawling on the sill.

When our art teacher asked the class to draw a corner of a room in our houses, all the others drew their sitting-rooms. I can still see the pictures pinned up on the art-room wall, the repeated grey pencil shading on televisions and sofas and armchairs and lamps. And I drew the boiler corner of the kitchen with its network of pipes, the improvised washing-lines strung with nappies, the one small galvanized radiator, the nursing-chair with its high wheel back and four short legs.

When John and I and the girls went on holiday, my parents sometimes came and stayed in our house. They would go shopping, or to the pictures. They would buy fish and chips and bring it back to eat at the kitchen table.

Once, when we got home, my father looked thoughtful. 'You know, I really like your house.'

'That's good,' I said. 'I'm glad.'

He went on, 'I really like your bathroom. I've been thinking what a nice bathroom you've got.'

'Our *bathroom*?'

After we'd said goodbye, I went up and stood staring at the bathroom, trying to see it through his eyes. It was – it still is – a supremely ordinary bathroom, small, white and pale blue, with a low ceiling. It is almost identical to his own bathroom, in fact.

When I go to the nursing-home to visit my father, there is sun falling on the new pink carpet, glinting on the wheelchairs and walking-frames. It is shining right in my father's eyes. I go to the window and pull the curtain across.

When I go upstairs to put something away in his room, I stop briefly on the landing to look out. You can see big old trees from there, and a wide lawn, and sky. From his room itself I look at it all again. It is as if he can't see it any more, and I have to see it for him. As if, without me, all that light would be wasted.

My father will refuse to have the cataract operations. 'Why would you want to put something in your eyes?' he will ask me. By the time my mother dies he will be quite blind.

That morning I shall go over to his house and draw back the curtains on a dazzle of honeysuckle full of bees. He will not be able to see it.

He will be upstairs, in the bedroom they shared. He will run his hands over her underwear, not quite cold, strewn across the furniture. 'Come on,' I shall say to him. 'You're coming to our house. I'm going to take you back with us.'

And I shall lead him down the stairs. He will be counting the treads. 'Come on,' I hear myself saying to him again. 'It's all right. I'll take care of you. You're my darling.' I lead him out over the threshold. 'Emily and Bridget are waiting for us,' I shall say.

My father and I would dig elaborate pools on the beach, fed by a complicated network of channels which tapped the natural streams that ran back towards the sea. Sometimes we would plan them on paper first. When the tide was right, we would spend all day digging. We would wait to see the sea reclaim them. When we got back to the caravan we would compare blisters.

*

My father never learned to swim. Once in a deep rocky pool somewhere in Cornwall his friends persuaded him to let them practise their life-saving skills. He almost drowned.

I didn't learn to swim until I was eleven. I was nervous of the water. 'How did you manage to learn?' I asked my mother.

'Oh . . .' She would shrug. 'When I was young, in Edenbridge, you never really had any chance *not* to learn. The boys picked you up and threw you in the river.' Later she would swim with me sometimes. I can see her wading carefully into the cold water. She had a navy-blue swimsuit printed all over with a pattern of enormous lobsters.

Now they tell me my father is to go to the day hospital twice a week. The ambulance will come and pick him up at the nursing-home in the morning and bring him back in the afternoon.

After his first visit I ask him how it went.

'All right,' he tells me. 'But I was sick on the way home. They went all round the houses.'

I commiserate. 'Did they say anything?' I ask him.

'Oh, the doctor gave me a good going-over. He tested my blood pressure. He made me move my knees.'

'And did he tell you anything?'

'No.'

'Didn't you ask him?'

'No.'

'Well, let's hope they can do something to make you feel . . .' I find myself at a loss.

After a few visits he tells me, 'The trouble is, they always make you sit around for so long, waiting. I have to wait a couple of hours sometimes after lunch, before they're ready to bring me home.'

'Do you wait somewhere comfortable?' I ask him. 'Can you doze off, while you're waiting?'

He shakes his head. 'You know what it's like. You can't really relax. You're afraid they'll forget about you, or something. And it's such a waste of time.'

I nod. 'What would you like to be doing with the time?' I ask him. I find myself wondering if I should take him there, twice a week, and bring him back as soon as the physiotherapy session is over. That way he wouldn't be sick. He wouldn't have to waste time.

A few weeks later they have signed him off. They have tried drugs, of various strengths, for pain, for arthritis, for Parkinson's disease, for depression. Nothing seems to make any difference. 'So you won't be having to go to the hospital any more,' I say to him. 'That's good. Now you won't have to sit about for hours, waiting.'

He looks at me sadly. 'We played bingo,' he says. 'While we waited. And the lunches were quite nice. Fish and chips we had, on Fridays. And mince. And apple pie, or rice pudding.'

My father was always mad on cars. He could list all the cars he had ever had, what colour they were, how many miles they had done when he bought them, how much he had paid for them. As you went back, the prices got crazier and crazier.

When I was nineteen he tried to teach me to drive. I remember learning to change gear on blind lanes with towering hedges.

Then he took me on a real road. I was stuck behind a tractor. Nothing was coming the other way. 'Overtake,' he said to me. Then, when I hung back, he said, 'Come on, overtake, silly!'

And somehow I brought the car to a stop and leaned forwards against the wheel. Then I started to scream.

Now I drive his car. He couldn't drive now without being a serious danger to someone. Yet the car is still insured only for himself and one other named driver.

Often he still says to me, 'I haven't driven for ages. It's going to feel really strange when I do. I hope I won't have lost my touch.'

'Where do you want to drive to?' I ask him, as I turn the key in the ignition.

He looks sideways at me. 'Oh, I don't know . . . To the shops, or the dentist. Or I might want to go and see someone. It feels odd not to have the car, when I might have to use it to go somewhere.'

'You know I'll always bring it if you need it,' I tell him. 'And then I'll be here anyway, to drive you.' I hesitate. 'How would you get into the car on your own? And how would you get from the car to where you were going?'

'Oh, I don't know . . . I'd manage.'

His right hand is resting absently on the gear-stick. I pick it up gently and move it to his knee.

She would drive back from the local hospital after a late shift, through dark, overgrown lanes. You could hear her coming for miles, the characteristic chug of her engine through silence.

'There was a man who drove a car. He took it to the garage, complaining that when he drove, there was a bad smell.

'The garage mechanic took the car out for a test-drive. He brought the car to a stop on the forecourt and got out. "I can't smell anything," he said.

' "Let me drive," the man said. "I'll show you."

'The two men got into the car and drove off. At first the man drove slowly. "Can you smell it?" he asked.

'The mechanic shook his head. "I can't smell anything."

'The driver speeded up. He was breaking the speed-limit. The mechanic found himself sweating. "Do you smell it now?" the man asked.

'Still the mechanic shook his head. "Are you sure there's a problem? I can't smell anything at all."

'Then the man drove like a madman. He took corners at seventy miles an hour, clipping the kerb. He almost ran down a child in a pushchair. He crunched to a halt an inch short of an articulated lorry. "*Now* do you smell it?" he asked.

' "Smell it? I'm *sitting* in it," the garage mechanic said.'

*

Now that it is summer, I begin to notice a bad smell in the car. At first it is only faint. Then it is more insistent. I open both front windows as wide as I can, but even the cross-breeze never seems quite to get rid of it. As soon as I stop, I find myself surrounded by the same invisible breath of decay.

I catch myself looking sideways at the front seat-covers, their fleecy fabric greyish, their pile flattened by a succession of drivers and passengers. This is where I have sat and sweated. This is where my father has sat sometimes in wet trousers to be driven home. 'Do these seat-covers come off?' I ask him.

'I don't know.' He looks at me blankly.

'I thought I might give them a wash,' I tell him.

But when I raise the driver's head-rest to find out how the cover is fastened, there is no zip, but only a line of my mother's careful stitching, like slightly uneven teeth.

I dream of body-parts, soft and spongy as if made of rubber. Dead, but still moving. On the ground they shake and squirm as if with life. I can hear them crying. And then they are gone. Emily and Bridget and I are standing there, looking at the ground.

And then that warmth, that hot, heavy, close warmth round my upper back and shoulders. And I realize the squashed limbs and fragments of limbs have crawled up under my sweatshirt. They are clinging to me. It is because I *know* them. They *know* me. It is because I have introduced myself to them. I have dared to touch them, to chop and punch at them, gouging them into dust like perished foam rubber. It is because I have dared to laugh.

I am protecting my daughters from dead limbs. I know they mustn't touch anything, mustn't be *recognized* by death. I tell them to stand back, well away. Away from the strewn limbs. Away from me.

Now my father has given Emily and Bridget all his old school prizes. 'Eric Wicks,' the plates say. 'Chemistry Prize', 'History Prize', 'Matriculation Prize, 1927'. Their titles make me smile: *Heroes of Greek Myth*, *The Lure of British Cathedrals*. But my daughters give them shelf space, with Robert Cormier and Colette.

My father would joke about handmaidens. 'I'm so tired,' he would say, as he got up to turn off the TV. 'Almost too tired to go to bed. All I want now is about a dozen handmaidens.'

My mother and I would laugh, exchanging glances.

'Two to carry me upstairs, two to do my teeth, two to undress me, two to fold my clothes, and two to . . .' Then he would reach out to both of us. 'But I've already got two lovely handmaidens,' he would say.

Each Sunday evening I push back the heavy doors and balance them open, the catch of the outer door just holding the inner door to make a clear path through. John steers my father into the lounge, where blue-uniformed nurses are moving about between the high-backed chairs. I lean over the wheelchair. 'Here are all your handmaidens,' I say into his ear. He looks up at me and half smiles.

My father's family was full of eccentrics. They became part of our family mythology in a way my mother's relatives never did. There was my father's Uncle Victor, who had always passed his young bride titbits from his own plate. Sometimes my mother would give me something from her own plate – a special sliver of chicken breast, a particularly succulent mushroom. 'Who do you think you are, Victor and Peggy?' my father would say.

In their youth Victor and Peggy used to ride a tandem. Peggy was tiny, a little birdlike figure. Once at some traffic-lights she dismounted and Victor rode on for miles without noticing she had gone.

My father's family was full of eccentrics. The most notable of them was his Uncle Walter. Quite suddenly, in his sixties, Uncle Walter had gone to bed. He had never got up again. He had simply decided to go to bed, and he stayed in bed for years, until the end of his life. Or at least, that was the way my father told it.

My father, whose second name was Eric, was named after him.

When my father goes into Greenfield House, I start to clear out his kitchen. On the worktop there is a plastic tub bursting with pieces of cut cardboard and tiny stubs of pencil sharpened at both ends. I keep about three sheets of card and two pencils and throw the rest away. Under the sink is a rusty tea-caddy full of string. Some of it is knotted together and wound into a ball. When I open the door of the larder, a plastic bag falls out on top of me, crammed with other plastic bags. I throw almost all of them away, half expecting to find them all folded one inside the other like Russian dolls.

When it is just beginning to get dark, you know because the lights begin to get brighter: car brake-lights, traffic-lights, the glow from windows. You can recognize the dark by the armbands of children. In the cave of the multi-storey car-park workmen stand in silver stripes, their bodies disappearing into a fluorescent exoskeleton of ribs.

My father had his two cataract operations on an out-patient basis. A nurse would come in to change the dressings. Then, for perhaps a year afterwards, he would have special eye-drops, which my mother administered.

When I opted for contact lenses, my parents were both aghast. 'Put something into your eyes?' My mother stared at me. 'But why on earth would you want to do that?'

He is getting slower and slower, later and later. Sometimes now when I come to collect him at midday on a Sunday he isn't ready. He has been awake since seven, but it takes him more than five hours now to have his breakfast and get dressed.

Usually I wait for him downstairs in the hall at Greenfield House. The nurses go up and chivvy him. Once Sister Latham said to me, 'I hope Eric won't think we're cruel, when we don't help him as much as he'd like us to. But we're still trying to get him to do as much for himself as he possibly can. The more we start doing for him, the more restricted his life is going to be.'

Once he takes so long I go up. He is standing in his pyjama trousers, leaning half on the Zimmer, half on the arm of the chair. He is just standing there crying. 'Come on,' I say. 'Our dinner'll be ready in half an hour. John'll wonder what's happened to us.' I go to his wardrobe. 'Which shirt do you want to wear?' I help him into it. We choose a tie and a cardigan. I help him into the wheelchair, and kneel down to push his feet into his shoes. It's not like putting on a child's shoes: his feet seem to be resisting me. His tears are dropping on my hands.

'You're wonderful. I don't know what I'd do without you,' he says.

Every time I ring the bell I notice the wisteria, like great knuckles up round the door and under his window. I dream of flying somewhere warmer, where the wisteria is already in full bloom, hanging like pale grapes in a sunlit hedge.

I dream that John, Emily, Bridget and I are on holiday somewhere in France. We are in the mushroom-coloured Mini we had thirteen or fourteen years ago, our first car. We are caught in a traffic-jam at the top of a hill, near the sea. I am wondering if I should get out with the children, for their sake, and take them to the beach for the day to play while John waits.

Then I seem to recognize one of the houses by the roadside. I get out of the car and wander across to the gate. I wade through the deep grass of an orchard until I am close enough to look through the windows. The simple interior is like a painting – old carved furniture, a check tablecloth, a bowl of glowing fruit. The windows all stand open on the dapple of summer light on grass. An old woman is working in the kitchen, wearing an old-fashioned flowered apron, the kind they used to wear in my childhood, just after the war. She is someone I know.

And then the traffic starts moving, and I am with the girls, walking downhill, then running, trying to find our car and get in. And then we are inside some kind of enclosed tunnel-like space, dark and steep. And people are passing back the word that they are having to load the cars quickly, a few at a time, and then move the boat in a few yards as the tide rises. And then suddenly the cars are all passing us in the other direction, driving back up and out, and someone is shouting, 'That's it! All get out now!' John must have driven the car up and out to safety because he is suddenly there with us, and we are all right, we are going to make it. The girls are running and he is pulling me by the hand and I am telling him to pull harder because my legs aren't working properly. I know it is because I am ill, but it doesn't matter, nothing matters, he is pulling me and we are all going to survive.

Some days now it hardly seems to get light.

I show my father my photograph in the paper, a group of poets grinning in the Poetry Society window. He goes straight back to his junk mail. I say, 'Which one is me?' He peers at the picture. 'That one.' He is pointing to someone else.

One of the Dr Barnardo's babies, Kevin, was almost a year old when he came to us. He was very unhappy. He would stand clinging to the furniture or the rim of the play-pen, his saucer eyes streaming tears. My parents were both distraught. All night he cried and cried and wouldn't be comforted, until finally they couldn't stand it any longer and took him under the covers with them. He butted his head hard into my mother's side and fell straight to sleep, as if he had only been waiting to share my parents' bed.

After that they shared their bed with him as often as they had to. He stayed with us for months. He started to talk. When my father was due back from London, Kevin would stand at the window watching for him. As soon as he caught sight of my father's neat trilby bobbing up the path, he would squeal, '*Dada!*' My father would scoop him up and hug him. They would go out

93

for drives, the two of them, Kevin sitting up in his car-seat in the front and waving goodbye to us like royalty.

Four or five years later his new parents brought him back to see us. He was called Brian by then. He clung to his new mother's hand and hid shyly in her skirts, eyeing my father's gleaming dark green Cortina in the front drive. He whispered something to his mother and she bent down to hear what it was. She looked embarrassed. 'Shhh,' she said.

Then he repeated it, more loudly, his small clear voice seeming to question all of us. 'Is that man going to take me out in his car?'

These days my father feels the cold terribly. Greenfield House is always wonderfully warm. When I go to see him, I peel off layers. When he comes to our house we have the central heating on as high as it will go. I light a fire in the sitting-room and put his chair close to it. But our house is old and draughty. When he wakes up from his nap he complains that his feet and hands are like ice.

My father and my mother both had ice-skates. They are still up there in that attic of his, in a labelled cardboard box, the black leather dry and cracking, the blades all rusty. One hard winter I got them out and tried them on. My father's feet were smaller than my mother's. I could pad his boots out with two pairs of thick socks. I smuggled them out of the house in a bag and taught myself to skate on a small isolated pond.

When my father comes to our house on Sundays he keeps asking us where the girls are. They come in and hug and kiss him. They show him their things, and ask him how he is. But between the roast and the pudding they go off to read for an hour, while John finishes the wine and I load the dishwasher. My father pauses between mouthfuls and looks up. 'Where are Emily and Bridget?' he says.

*

When I had Emily, my mother delved in one of her cupboards and brought out a huge pile of nappies. She had been saving them for me for almost twenty years.

Our house was always full of the stuff my mother would get from the clinic – bottles of concentrated orange juice, tins of Cow & Gate, monster jars of Marmite. Our house was always full of other people's babies. My mother had an old-fashioned pair of cast-iron baby-scales with a wicker basket. When Emily was born they became mine.

After his visits to the day hospital my father is referred to a psychologist. She is called Nicola. I imagine her young and pretty.

Every week she visits him, on a Tuesday. They talk for an hour. 'What do you talk to her about?' I ask him.

'Oh, you know. We just chat. About the past, mostly.'

'About Mum?'

'Yes. I suppose so. And about the house, and the old days. About when my mother died.'

'And does it help? Does it make you feel better to talk to her?'

He considers for a moment. Then he says, 'I do enjoy her visits. She's very sweet.' He breaks off again, thinking. 'Nicola's a very sweet girl,' he says.

'Nicola says he's still grieving,' Sister Latham tells me.

This is no news to me.

But she goes on. 'Not just about his wife, but about his house. And he's still unhappy about losing his own mother.'

'That was thirty years ago,' I say.

She shakes her head. 'I know. But Nicola says he still muddles them up sometimes.'

When Nicola's visits are due to come to an end, Sister Latham calls me into the office. 'It's her last visit next week,' she says.

'I know. He told me. She wrote all the dates down for him on a piece of paper.'

95

Sister Latham picks up a pen from the desk and turns it in her fingers. 'Nicola says he ought to be angry. When counselling is withdrawn, the client is supposed to get angry. That's part of the pattern, a stage they go through.'

'He's not angry,' I say. 'He's just sad. A bit sadder than usual.'

'Nicola says that's part of the trouble – that he's never been able to get angry. He should have felt hostile towards his wife for having died and left him.'

I smile ruefully. 'Can I be angry for both of us?' I say.

When Emily was a toddler, she had a word for us both. She would look at me hopefully. 'Mumily go out?' she would say.

When my father drove us down to Little Common for the summer holidays, we would stop and have our sandwiches on Ashdown Forest, even though the picnic spot was only a few miles away from where we had started. It was a ploy to stop me from being sick.

Then we would go on, down past the sign that said, 'Duck Eggs'. 'I don't know why they still insist on throwing all these eggs across the road!' my father always said.

If I lay down flat on the back seat I could stop myself feeling sick. I could look up and see branches going over my head. It was like being in a pram. Or I would open my back window as far as it would go and hang my head out. When I took my head in again, my face would be cold, dead as a mask.

When Emily was small, she used to dance round me as I pushed Bridget in the buggy, overtaking me first on one side and then on the other, stepping sideways, laughing, doubling back. Her fine hair would blow straight up from her head in wisps. One moment I would catch her skipping shadow over my hands, and then she would be gone, somewhere behind me. Then I would feel her tugging at my coat.

'Excuse me. Can I live with you?'

'Who are you?'

'I am the hysteria fairy.'

'The *what*?'

'The hysteria fairy.'

'Wisteria,' I said. 'Wist, like witch, whimsical, whisper.'

'Can I live with you?'

She would look at me gravely, waiting for an answer. Suddenly I would want to kiss or shake her. 'That depends.'

'What does it depend on?'

'Well, will you like us? Will we like you? What about my other daughter?' I would make a gesture towards the small shape slumped in the pushchair. 'Will there be enough room for you where we live?'

And Emily would make me describe it all in detail, the house, the garden, her bedroom, her toys, the lopsided animals made out of toilet-roll tubes and tissue paper. When I had finished she would nod and prompt me. 'Which is very lucky, because . . .'

'Which is very lucky because I had a daughter just like you who ran away this morning. She was exactly the same size as you are. You can have all the things she left behind. You can even eat what I was going to give her for her tea. I hope you like the same things as she did.'

She would frown. 'I may do. I may not.'

'What do you mean, you may not?' I pretend to be indignant.

'Fairies aren't like humans. They don't have mothers and fathers. They don't always like what humans like.'

'How do they feel about ice-cream?' I would ask her.

Often I sit with my father while he dozes. I do piles of mending, sew on name-tapes, write letters. Emily is out with her friends. Bridget is playing pretend-games in the garden, or in her room. My father opens his eyes and looks at me as I sit sewing. I know that for a moment he sees my mother. Then he says, 'Where are the girls?'

'Did they tell you about poor Mrs Blackford?' my father asks me.

It is September. We are sitting in the lounge, he in his faded pink wing-chair, I on a dining-chair pulled up to his elbow.

97

Around us the small semicircle of residents seems unnaturally depleted. 'What about Mrs Blackford?' I ask him.

'She died.'

'Oh. I'm sorry. When?'

'I don't know. Last week sometime.'

'She wasn't . . . I mean . . .' I try to find the right words. Out of the corner of my eye I still seem to see the familiar shape standing hunched at the French doors, the haggard face staring out over the line of parked cars, towards the high trees beyond. She is still calling, 'Hilary! *Hilary!*' in that same cracked, urgent voice.

We are quiet for a moment. Then my father says, 'This is the time of year, you know.'

'What do you mean?'

'When they all start to pop off. Just at the end of the winter.'

'It isn't the end of the winter,' I tell him. 'It's only just the beginning of the autumn.'

He glosses it over. 'Well . . . the turn of the year, anyway. That's when they all start to go.'

I fold his newspaper up carefully and lean across him to put it down on the table, next to his forgotten cup of tea. 'You aren't . . . worrying about it, are you?' I ask him.

'No. Oh, no.' He turns his head to look at me and smiles faintly. 'She wasn't anything to me. And I suppose, in a place like this . . . I don't really worry about it much at all.'

'Good,' I say. 'You shouldn't.' I change the subject. 'You haven't told me about the outing yesterday. Did you get to see the reservoir? Did they take you down to the water?'

He shakes his head. 'No. I didn't actually get as far as the water. But it was very nice. We had crisps, and sausage rolls. They'd done it all very nicely.'

I squeeze his hand. 'Good,' I say again. 'I'm glad.'

'It's ages since I'd been to Bewl Bridge.'

'Yes. It must be. When was the last time?'

'Oh . . .' He tries to remember. 'Not for ages. Not since they first built the dam.'

*

As I get up to go, he says, 'Tell the girls I'm going to take them.'

'Emily and Bridget?'

'Yes. The girls. Tell them I'm going to drive them out to Bewl Bridge next summer. When the nice weather comes.'

I kiss him on the cheek as usual. 'I will,' I say. 'I'll tell them as soon as I get home.'

My mother learned most of what she knew about mothering from my father's mother. Not having had the experience of a mother of her own, she learned to cook, clean, care for her man from the one woman who had cared for him best. She learned to make roasts and gravy, stuffing and vegetables, pastry and puddings, to the exact specifications of his personal preference.

He would never let her make him curry. She made that occasionally for herself, and later for me, but it was always considered too spicy and foreign for my father. 'But you used to eat curry sometimes, when your mother made it!' she would exclaim in good-humoured exasperation.

Once, on her birthday, we took them out for a meal in an Indian restaurant. My mother shone with the pleasure of it, tasting everything. My father had steak and chips. And my mother treated him like a hero.

My father keeps my first book of poems on his bedside table. He has never read any of it. He has never mentioned any of the poems to me. He never gets past the dedication. He shows the nurses the dedication, and cries.

On the wall, just to the left of my feet, my dentist has a picture of wisteria. Towards the bottom of the twig there is a small brownish bird that appears to be a wren. She is tiny, as long as two flower-buds, dwarfed by the purple profusion.

For a long time my dentist looks into my mouth, wiping and rewiping the mist of my breath from his little mirror. Finally he says, 'Just a couple of quickies I really ought to do today. You

99

won't even feel them. You won't need an injection. We're lucky this time. The tooth's dead.'

For years before my mother died my father never seemed to listen to any of us. He was always waiting to take over the conversation with an anecdote of his own.

Yet later we would hear him telling someone else what we had just said to him. And he would be able to repeat it all, almost word for word.

Whenever we went over to my parents' house for lunch on a Sunday, my mother would be in the kitchen, making gravy or timing vegetables. She would dish up and expect us to start without her, while the food on our plates was still hot.

We would tell my father something. He would seem barely to hear us. And she would appear in the doorway in a cloud of steam, as if by magic. 'Do *listen* to this, Eric! Do take it in. I don't want to miss any of their news! Then you can tell me it all afterwards.'

By the time she could join us my father was telling one of his stories.

My father wasn't the only one to have got a scholarship to the grammar school a year early: my mother had done the same. She had been good at maths. In the sixth form she had studied advanced maths and cookery. When she decided to be a nanny, her teachers tried to dissuade her.

But what she remembered were the failures. 'My English is "no better than that of a child of the Lower Third!" ' she would tell us, smiling. 'You know it's too deep for me.'

When people asked me which of my parents I preferred, I always said my father.

No one could write now in this room. The worn grey carpet needs replacing; the cheap ready-made curtains remind you of bed and breakfast places. His old office typewriter still sits on the table I sat at to revise for my O-levels, thirty years ago.

The twin beds are pushed together, but only one of them is made. The little French-polished mahogany table on his side is scarred by screw-holes, where he fixed an improvised bracket for his reading-lamp. Both beds are strewn with his papers, the old unused manila envelopes he has collected over the years, the obsolete business paper with the firm's heading cut off. In the corner by the cupboard there is a high pile of cereal packets – Shredded Wheat, Corn Flakes, Rice Krispies – as if he were expecting some disaster. My mother's underwear still slung across the back of a chair.

These are his clothes. His old winter trousers. The dress-suit trousers he used to wear to play his dance music in, frayed at the waist, the turn-up creases disappearing into loose dark threads. The cardigan my mother has knitted new sleeves on, the two greens of her wool not quite matching. The bedsocks in strange colour combinations – red, olive, pink, ecru. The holes that let the colour of his toes poke through. Should I darn them, as she did? And if I should darn them, what colour wool should I use?

My friends always wanted to come and stay at our house. My parents gave me a lot of freedom. When my friend Catherine came, she borrowed an old pair of jeans of mine and some Wellington boots. We spent a blissful weekend damming a stream, covering ourselves with mud and slime, wearing our fingernails right down to the quick.

When I went to stay for a reciprocal weekend at her house, we said grace before meals and visited the museum.

My French penfriend, Arlette, could make my father angry. Once, when she and her brother were fighting in the back of the car, my father stopped dead and refused to drive any further until they were quiet. '*Shut UP!*' he shouted at them, and they did.

*

101

Arlette was having trouble sleeping. She was anxious about her school-work. She became obsessed with the shape of her own body, climbing on chairs to look at her thighs in the mirror over the fireplace.

My parents watched, full of anxiety. Then one morning my father said, 'That's enough!'

He went out into the hall. We could hear him using the phone. He had booked Arlette on the first flight back to Paris. I think she hugged him. She loved them both. She loved him all the more for sending her away.

My friends sometimes told me how lucky I was. 'Your parents are so lovely!' they would say. 'You can always say anything to them. You can tell them anything you like.'

It has snowed. The winter footprints of birds are like stars, or arrows. They lead to the very coldest place, where there is no food for them at all.

When my father was here he would always feed the birds. He would put out his scraps on the patio, not just crumbs and bacon fat, but chicken bones with gravy, leftover shepherd's pie, anything. Perhaps the rats came and took it. Perhaps the birds really did eat it. But anyway, he would go on putting it all out, and by the next day it would all have disappeared.

One of my father's principal hobbies was lighting bonfires. He and my mother would pile the damp garden waste in a huge stack and burn it as slowly as possible, wrapping the whole neighbourhood in a pall of smoke.

He would come down in the morning to see a wisp of thin smoke still rising and he would go outside to poke at the pile with a garden fork. He would come back rubbing his hands. 'How would you like that lot down the back of your trousers?' he would say to us.

On my birthday I would have a bonfire party, with baked potatoes and sausages. My father would light the fireworks one by one, at a safe distance. One year he made me a guy, a wooden structure jointed at the hip and knee, shoulder and elbow, like a real man. We dressed it together in his old clothes. We put fireworks in its pockets.

John holds the ladder while I ease myself up rung by rung. Under me the aluminium of the extension gives slightly and settles into place until the catch clicks. I stand in the square hole and reach for the light.

Containers surround me at eye-level: cardboard boxes, old biscuit-tins with scratched lids, a wooden chest, a graduated row of suitcases. I pull myself up into the hole and try to read the descriptions of their contents: 'racquets, shuttlecocks, ice-skates' in my father's small, regular copperplate; 'patterns from Freda', 'jamjars', 'curtains' in my mother's schoolgirl script.

A small black case catches my eye and I open it. Inside the separate pieces of a clarinet lie in plum-coloured velvet. A tarnished key is sellotaped to the outside. Next to the case there is a small polythene package gathered at the waist by a rubber band. I go to open it and the band disintegrates against my fingers with a snap. The polythene under it is half opaque with years of creases. I reach inside and take out a pair of beaters, the wooden handles slightly warped, the small dark rubber heads bound in bottle-green wool, their impact muted by my mother's aching fingers.

In my mind's eye I can still see him, the winding country road he is following, the tree-trunks pale in the beam of his headlights, the moon glimpsed between high hedges. And the policeman at the car window, scanning documents with his torch. 'What's your business tonight, sir? Would you mind telling us your destination? And the identity of your passenger?'

We used to laugh at that, imagining the lumpy features of the vibraphone in its canvas carrying-case, erect on the front passenger seat. 'And how did you answer?' I would ask my father.

Now I find myself smiling as I balance the smooth wood of the beaters across my hands and feel the weight of the heads, slightly perished under my mother's patient green stitching. I reach out and try a short snatch of rhythm on a nearby suitcase. From the hollow sound it makes I can tell there is nothing inside.

As a small child I was always dreaming there were ants in my bed. My mother would come in and turn on the light and strip off the bedclothes. 'Look, darling, no ants! Not a single one!' And I would look and still see them swarming across the white sheet. Then gradually my eyes would get used to the light and I would see there really was nothing there.

My parents would half joke about death. One summer they wore themselves out sorting through boxes of old stuff in the attic. They looked at me oddly, smiling like conspirators. 'Better to do it now, rather than leave it for you to do, when we're *gone* . . .'

One day I shall go and live in their empty house. I will live in it as they lived in it, economizing on hot water by using the water-heater over the sink, saving bottle tops and plastic bags, cutting up cereal packets to write my lists on. I shall spend my evenings in front of the television. Then I shall go upstairs to sleep with an old sock full of corks.

At the moment she dies I am seven miles away, sitting in my sunlit garden, reading Flaubert. My sun-hat is pulled down over my eyes. The sun is so bright that even with sun-glasses I am squinting at the glare from the white table, the white page. And seven miles away she is lying on a sofa, and she dies. I brush crumbs from the spine of my book, and turn the page.

My mother said to us once, 'I think it's terrible, the way these marriages break up, and the wife runs home to her parents.'
John looked at her and said gravely, 'Well, Joy, if *our* marriage breaks up, *I'll* be the one to come back and live with you. Is that all right?'

*

From here it seems more beautiful than any kite I have ever imagined, the tiny square face bobbing at the end of the long arc of string, the tail-bows glittering as they ripple in air currents higher and colder than ours. 'Can I hold it?' I shall beg him.

'I'm not sure you're strong enough, darling. It's very fierce.'

He will make me stand in the span of his arms, closed in front by the stick of string and behind me by the wind-shadow of his body. I shall put my hands between his bigger ones at either end of the spool and he will relax his arms slightly to let me feel the kite's pull. 'Gosh.' Even in the shelter of his chest my two pigtails will rise and flick forwards over my shoulders. Little wisps of hair will pull out of the slide and blow across my line of vision. My skirt will be flapping against the backs of my knees.

'Don't let go,' he will warn me as the kite snakes in a stronger gust. But I needn't worry: he will still be holding the ends of the stick firmly.

After a while I shall duck down and scamper out from between his arms.

From outside in my back garden I can see the kids who live in one of the houses that back on to ours. They sit in the open sash window, smoking, their legs hanging over the sill, their feet touching the sloping roof of the kitchen. It is that moment of the evening when the cold air outside meets the warm air of a room and you feel you could walk on unlikely surfaces – or dance. The music your parents hate is blaring out behind you, cutting you off from them, from your brothers and sisters, from everything, floating in the winter dusk like good news.

I was a student in Provence when my parents drove down to Montpellier with Harry and Mona to pick up the caravan. I had no money. I asked them if I could cadge a lift back.

My uncle's car wasn't insured for my father to drive. My aunt wasn't driving either. And my uncle was ill, suffering from stomach-cramps and lack of sleep. As he drove on to a round-about at Soissons we were all straining to read the signs.

Before we knew it a van came shooting at us from the right. I saw it coming. I saw it was going to hit us. I heard my mother scream. It hit us hard across the front, on the driver's side. Then it seemed to lift into the air. It turned right over and landed on its roof, by the side of the road.

'*Dead.*' The word flashed across my eyes. But as we stared, a side door grated open and a man clambered out. Then he ran across to us and stuck his hand through the open window. He shook hands vigorously with my uncle, then with the rest of us. He was grinning.

But my mother was hysterical. She was sobbing over and over again, 'Mona, *Mona!* What's happened to Mona? *Mona!*'

My father put his arm round her shoulders. '*She's all right! Darling. Listen to me. It hit us on Harry's side and Susan's, not on Mona's. Mona's all right. Not even a scratch. Look.*'

Already the police were on the scene. I had started to shake. '*Il paraît que vous parlez français.* Can you tell us exactly what happened?' someone said.

I travelled from Aix-en-Provence to spend the weekend with my parents and aunt and uncle in Montpellier. They spent the days sitting in the scrubby little garden, reading. In the evening they played cards. For once my father had no car. He was feeling restless. 'Let's go out for the day,' I said to him.

'Where could we go?'

'We'll get on a bus,' I told him. 'There's something I've been wanting to look at.'

It was a clear hot day. We caught the bus to Sète and found our way to the cemetery. We climbed about between the terraced graves. It was lunch-time. The marble tombs glared. Everything – the gravel, the bleached grass, our own hot feet – seemed thirsty for shadow. We sat down, squinting at the glittering roof of the sea.

On the way home we were sharing a bag of cherries on our laps when a gang of youths got on and sat at the back of the bus. They must have been drunk. They were laughing and jeering, taunting the driver, shouting obscenities. The driver remonstrated. They went on shouting. Then we heard him say something quietly, as if under his breath.

A couple of kilometres further on the bus stopped. Suddenly we were surrounded by sirens and flashing blue lights. A posse of gendarmes crashed up the aisle, grabbed the kids by the scruff of their necks and hustled them out by the rear door. Then the driver calmly restarted the engine, glancing once in his rear-view mirror as we lumbered out again into the traffic. I looked at my father. He winked at me. The cherries were nearly all gone, the brown paper shredding between our fingers with dark juice.

Later that night he told the others the story. Where we had gone. What we had seen. He hardly mentioned our pilgrimage. But the youths on the bus, the driver, the gendarmes with their grim faces – he told all that in minute detail, marvelling.

And even now he still likes to think of it. 'Do you remember when we went to the cemetery at Sète?' I sometimes ask him.

His loose face lifts in a slow smile. 'Those yobs on the bus! And those French gendarmes!' He chuckles. 'They don't put up with any nonsense, do they, over there in France!'

My father began to go grey when he was still at school; by the time I was born he was almost completely silver. Then as the years went by the grey bleached gradually to white. My mother and I would tell him he looked very distinguished. He would smile his little-boy smile. 'Fair,' he would correct us. 'I've always been fair. I'm getting fairer all the time.'

One afternoon at Greenfield House Bridget and I go upstairs together to fetch my father's glasses. At the top the fire-door swings open and I see Mavis, bent over her Zimmer. I hear her ask in her quavering old woman's voice, 'Oh! Have you come to take me down? I . . . I've been . . . waiting . . . I've been waiting here since . . .'

Bridget hesitates. Then she says, 'I expect someone's coming to help you in a minute.'

My daughter stands there, just in front of me, slim and straight in her jeans and T-shirt, her fair hair hanging down between her shoulder-blades in a fat plait. 'Oh!' Mavis says again. She looks at Bridget more closely. 'Are you a new resident?'

One Sunday afternoon I am sitting with my father as he dozes. I am taking the blue name-tapes off Emily's outgrown school blouses and re-marking them with Bridget's red ones. I am sewing new blue name-tapes on to a pile of new bigger blouses for Emily. From time to time I glance up from threading the needle and see my father slightly slumped in his chair, his chin on his chest, his pink crown shining through the thin strands of his silver hair.

Then, as I am still sewing, I hear a strange sound, a sort of sloshing. I peep up at him and see him out of the corner of my eye. There is a row of false teeth in his lap. As I watch, he lifts it in both hands and tries to put it back into his mouth. The saliva sloshes, and dribbles down. I bend my head again over my sewing, not letting him see I have noticed.

But the noise continues. Five minutes. Ten. I glance at the clock on the mantelpiece. And when I next look up, there is not one row of teeth, but two, a whole disembodied smile parting against the damp folds of his trousers.

One morning after a dance he handed me a box. I reached out awkwardly and took it. I looked at him.

'Be careful. It might jump out and hit you on the nose!'

I held the box at arm's length and opened it as slowly as I could. The thin white cardboard lid gave under the pressure and came up suddenly in my hand. I reached down with my fingers. There seemed to be nothing inside. Then, right at the bottom, I felt something hard and complicated. I put my hand all the way in and brought out the thing I had felt. It was a sugar rose. Its stiff pink petals shook slightly on my palm.

'It's from the top of the cake. I told them about you and they said I could have it.' He was half propped on an elbow, looking at me, the top buttons of his pyjama jacket undone and the smooth pale skin of his chest showing. 'What's the matter? Don't you like it?'

'It's lovely,' I said. 'Thank you.'

I took it to my bedroom and set it carefully on the mantelpiece on a square of smoothed-out silver paper. Between the scars of old wrinkles I could just make out a second rose, the inverted reflection of curling outer petals. From week to week the two flowers slowly gathered dust, changing from pink to off-white, and then unambiguously to grey, until one afternoon I reached out, broke off a petal and put it to my tongue. It tasted of sweet dust. I opened the window and leaned over the sill to spit it out into the garden. Then I locked myself in the lavatory with what was left. I broke each brittle curl into fragments and saw them sink like gravel to lie close together, cupped in white porcelain. I watched them as I pulled the chain.

I let the kite go, his perfect gift to me. I let the string burn me and slip through my fingers. 'You *chump*!' was what he called me. 'All my hard work! Didn't you realize what a pull it had?'

I can still see the three of us struggling against the wind and the uneven ground as we made our way back to the car. I was crying silently. My mother walked behind us with the bag. My father's angry back went on ahead, his open raincoat flapping as he got out his keys and bent to unlock the door.

Just once, as he turned the key in the ignition, I risked a question. 'Perhaps those people who were out in the boats might have . . . ?'

He turned his head to look at me and gave a short laugh.

'Shhh.' My mother was handing me a bun. 'Don't go on about it, Eric. You can make her another one. You enjoyed making it. You know you did.'

He laughed again, the same laugh, as the car swung into the coast road, tyres crunching on gravel. 'I'm blowed if I'm going to waste my time and money on a bit of rubbish for her to throw into the sea!'

Every time my father mentions my mother he cries. He steers the conversation to a point where he can talk about her. But he never does talk about her. He sobs and mops his eyes with one of his grubby frayed handkerchiefs. Six months ago he would stand in the kitchen of his house and cling to me, as tears splashed on to the grey and yellow tiles.

But for once he mentions her and smiles, his eyes full of tears. And the conversation moves on.

I dream that my mother is alive. I dream that she is here. She has been ill. She's had some kind of stroke or heart attack. She's not allowed to do any chores or run round after us. And I keep thinking, 'Why can't my father accept it? Why can't he accept just her presence and be happy, without needing her to look after him?' And then I find myself thinking, 'But perhaps he *will*. Perhaps one day soon he *will*!'

When John goes away, my father misses him. He tells me he misses him. Five minutes later he tells me again. He looks up at Emily and Bridget. 'I hope your two manage to find themselves such good husbands,' he says to me. 'I hope they give you such wonderful sons-in-law, to look after you in your old age.'

My father's idea of gardening was to walk about slowly on the back lawn, stopping here and there to pick up a stone or a bit of stick. While my mother pruned or weeded, he would spend hours picking up chips of stone or brick which he piled in little cairns on the crazy paving.

After my mother died, he would stop whatever he was doing to bend down and pick up a crumb from the carpet. When he comes to our house for lunch on a Sunday, he will suddenly disappear under the table for several minutes to pick up a pea or a scrap of paper.

*

Now the grass is coming up through the crazy paving in great clumps, because he hasn't walked there. The front drive is green with moss. Indoors there are cobwebs, invisible grey strands strung right across the hall to brush your face as you go past. There are cobwebs in the corners, the wrapped dead bodies of nameless, formless things in soft grey pellets. I try to clean the white spots off the furniture. The duster comes away with a long thin beard of grey dust.

One day I shall go and live in their empty house. I will live in it as they lived in it, mastering the heavy Flymo and the feeble vacuum cleaner that seems to blow out more dust than it sucks in. I shall spend hours in the kitchen, seeing the trees through a film of steam. I shall poke the churning mass in the twin-tub with long wooden tongs.

Just before she died my mother told me how they had brought her mother home from the hospital once, as an experiment. How she and Mona had hidden in the cupboard under the stairs. How frightened they had been.

My mother told me about the lie she had told, as a child. How they had set fire to the haystack and gone home to hide. And how the policeman had questioned them afterwards. And what she had said.

My parents were always completely honest. I can't think of a single lie they ever told me. They told me about Father Christmas, but they told me he wasn't real. They were afraid I would have nightmares about men coming down my chimney.

This year we can't take him on holiday with us. We have let it go, let him carry on half believing that he will still come with us. But we can't do it. We are renting a caravan in Devon. I imagine us helping him up the steps, supporting him under the arms as he takes a shower. I see him with his walking-frame, blocking the gangway between the table and the stove. In memory I measure the impossible steep distance from the car-park to the beach; I watch the girls kick off their sandals and run off to look at the rock-pools. I hear his little voice in my ear, asking if he can go home.

But we haven't told him. We've let it go. This Sunday lunchtime I know that I must tell him the truth.

I drive him up through the sleepy town centre as usual. Up Mount Pleasant to Fiveways. I stop at a red light. 'You know, I don't think it's going to work,' I say.

He looks at me mildly.

'The holiday,' I tell him. 'In the caravan. I don't think we're going to be able to take you. I don't see how we can manage.'

There is a silence. Then he says, 'I suppose I *am* a bit of an encumbrance. I can quite see how you wouldn't want to be bothered with an old crock like me.'

I don't know what to say to him. 'It's just that . . .' I cobble together excuses. 'You know it's no reflection on . . . You know how much . . .'

His face these days is almost always impassive. But he says, 'I know, darling. No one could have such a lovely family as I have, such a lovely daughter.'

I blink back tears as I still look at the hooded light. I realize that for some moments already it has been green.

The day before we leave I take my father to the dentist. I allow well over an hour to drive him the six miles from the nursing-home.

I park in the village square and wheel him up along the pavement to the surgery. The receptionist helps me negotiate the high concrete step into the waiting-room. Later, when he comes out of the dentist's room, I hear the same kindly receptionist asking him for his new address. I hear his voice telling her, with pauses as she writes it down. The address is a complete fabrication, some waste-product thrown out by his imagination. As tactfully as I can, I tell her the right one. I almost wonder if I am

112

the one who is hallucinating, visiting him among the ruined walls of some house that has never existed. He seems so reasonable. But she is used to these things. She is only mildly surprised.

She helps me lift him in the wheelchair backwards down the surgery steps. I push him back down the irregular brick pavement, down awkward kerbs and up on the other side, to the car. As I struggle to get him smoothly into his front passenger seat, a man rushes out from the off-licence to help me, with what feels like exaggerated *bonhomie*. I fold the wheelchair and lift it into the boot, leaning it at just the right angle so it won't rattle. I slam the boot shut and close his door gently. I open my own, slide into the driving seat, close the door, fasten his seat-belt for him. I fasten my own. I check the mirror, and turn the key in the ignition.

'I'm afraid I just need to go to the Gents for a moment,' he says.

I keep my face and voice quite steady. 'I wish you'd said.'

'I didn't need to go, before. I just want to go now, quickly.'

I don't sigh. I lean over and stroke his hand. I unfasten my belt and his. I get out of the car and go round to open the boot. I lift out the wheelchair and press down hard on the sides of the seat until it opens.

We spend a week in a rented cottage near Worcester. When we visit Worcester Cathedral I ask to be allowed to see the misericord that tells the story of the clever daughter. An obliging woman looks up the number in some kind of catalogue. A man in black clothes takes me to the choir-stalls and lifts a seat to reveal the carving underneath. I creep under the rope and sit where no one can see me. He tells me to be discreet and replace the seat when I leave. Otherwise all the schoolkids will be always noisily flipping the seats and breaking them. Bits of priceless carving will drop off.

I crouch there on the bare wooden steps, and the clever daughter looks back at me, her narrow eyes peering at me from under her high forehead, the lower part of her face blurred, eaten away by wear. She is very ugly. One enormous splayed foot rests on the ground, between the legs of the ram. The other is high

113

against the animal's flank, held in a broad stirrup. Her right hand is resting on curved horn.

She is dressed in a short cloak of coarse netting. The lozenge-shaped gaps between the threads are half as big as her hand. Four of them would cover her face. Under the cloak she appears to be naked. Her left arm cradles the hare like an extra breast. It takes me a while to make out its long ears. For a moment I think it is a part of her own body.

Clothed and unclothed, riding and not riding. The gift that cannot be given.

She looks intelligent. But she looks strained and stiff, caught for ever in her pose of clever paradox. Only the hare is warm. Under the netting its small head droops towards her right elbow as if it could travel there, half hidden against her left breast, for ever.

Emily and Bridget and I were walking home from school in the rain. I can still see Bridget's plump legs reflected upside down in the puddles as she stopped to pull up her long navy-blue socks. They were both holding my hands as we struggled across the road, loaded with shopping and satchels and lunch-boxes. We kept tripping over one another. It was like an odd kind of six-legged race, which no one ever quite lost or quite won.

My arms were aching. 'Not far now,' I told them, squeezing the little warm fingers.

Then an ambulance rushed past us, wailing, flashing its lights. The cars gave way and it rushed into the hole between them and nothing was left behind. The cars and lorries and bicycles nosed out into the road again. 'Someone must have needed help quickly,' I said. A crash victim? Stroke? Heart attack? A would-be suicide discovered at the last possible moment, a marginal case? 'Someone's had an accident,' I said.

Emily considered it for a moment. Then she agreed with me. 'Yes. I expect you're right, Mummy. The pavements *are* very slippery.'

*

114

I shall move out of here and go and live in my parents' empty house. There is no one there now, only dust. I can be on my own there all day.

And little by little I'll change it. I'll put away the woven plastic mats in the kitchen, the transparent runner in the hall. I'll throw away the padded silk *Mona Lisa*, the donkey with the panniers, the margarine tub of water on the hearth. I'll lift the carpets and re-wax the floors, buy rugs in jewel colours. I'll repaint everything. I'll get rid of the secondary aluminium double glazing, the pink and mauve candlewick bedspreads, the TV, the soap-clogged steel basket over the bath. I'll open all the windows and turn up the heat. I'll knock down the wall between the dining-room and the kitchen.

We were making plans to spend a year in the United States. 'We might not be here when you get back,' my father said to us one day.

They were both in good health. 'Where are you expecting to go?' I asked him.

'Well.' He coughed. 'We might be . . . you know.'

'If either of you were ill,' I told him, 'we'd come back. You know we would.'

'But we might just . . . pop off.'

There was a silence. Then John said, deadpan, 'Let's get this straight, Eric. What you'd really like us to do is to pitch a tent on your front lawn and camp here permanently, waiting for you to die?'

My mother giggled. 'Oh, John. You *are* silly!' She always called him silly. It meant he knew how to make her laugh.

We are coming home. I recognize the sinking feeling as we drive up from the coast. We are caught behind a tractor with a trailer stacked high with bales of straw. For miles we follow it through sun and shadow, as the overhanging branches brush straw from the stack, showering us with gold needles. The yellow dust swirls on the tarmac in front of us, spinning into the light when we finally manage to overtake.

*

115

One Sunday my father locks himself in the toilet. After half an hour he still hasn't emerged. We begin to feel concerned. 'Are you all right in there, Eric?' John calls through the door.

'Well . . . I *shall* be all right in a minute. I'm just . . .' The voice tails off.

'Just what?'

'Just stuck for the moment. I'll be out in a minute or two.'

'Don't worry,' we tell him. 'Just try to get yourself up so you can unlock the door.'

We go downstairs and wait. We try to decide how long to give him before breaking the door down. We settle on another half-hour.

When the half-hour is up, I go upstairs to see if he has made any progress. I take one stair at a time, not looking ahead. But when I get to the top, he is standing there behind his Zimmer-frame in the doorway, smiling at me.

'Oh!' I say. I take a deep breath. 'Well done! You managed.'

He grunts. 'I'm afraid I've made a bit of a mess of your lavatory. Those toilet-roll holders are very flimsy.'

'Don't worry about that,' I tell him. 'That's trivial. I was just afraid you were really trapped.' I follow the long white ribbon of paper and pick it up. Then I fetch a dustpan and brush from the hall cupboard and get down on my hands and knees.

One day he will remember me when he is out playing at a dance and bring me something – a balloon, a streamer, a decorated paper napkin. I shall crawl into bed with him the next morning and he will say sleepily, 'I've got something for you. You see my jacket hanging on the chair over there? If you look in the left-hand pocket . . .' And I shall look, and find some little treasure, a talisman from the place where they dance until midnight.

He will hand me a plain white box.

I shall look at him, afraid to open it.

'Be careful. It might jump out and hit you on the nose!'

I shall hold the box at arm's length and try to lift the lid slowly. But somewhere inside it a catch will click and an invisible spring

116

will jerk the lid open. A little red and yellow man will bounce to and fro, grinning at me. His stiff hair will stand up all over his head. 'Where did you get him?' Do the couples who dance until midnight play with toys?

He will laugh at my face. 'It was a prize. I won it in the raffle. You can have it.'

I shall bring the Jack-in-the-box back into my father's warm bed, amusing myself by pressing on the top of the little wooden head until I can fasten the catch, then opening the lid and letting it spring out again. I aim the box at my father, then at myself. I shall even try it under the bedclothes. In the end I shall leave him to sleep and carry the closed box carefully back to my own room. I shall stand it on the window-sill, where I can let the little man out at a touch.

Several times, as I was growing up, my father's mother was mentally ill. He used to tell me occasionally about the worst time, the time he visited her and she didn't even know him. And I would try to feel as he must have felt. For your parents not to know you seemed more terrible than anything else I could imagine.

But one day I shall open the heavy double doors and walk through to where he is sitting, and he will look up at me and not know who I am. And I will go up to him and hug him as usual. And it will be a relief.

One day I shall drive his car home, to where I grew up. I shall take the old turning, back to Staffords Wood. I'll follow a track to a little clearing, beech and hazel branches closing behind me. I'll turn off the engine and get out. I'll breathe in the damp, half-remembered smell of leaves. I'll watch a coin of sunlight move on the car's bonnet. I'll open the boot and get out a length of hose.

As I open the car door and slide into the driver's seat, I'll hear birds singing. I'll look again at the car, the outside with its two small dents, one his, one mine. The inside with its rucked fleecy covers and pockets stuffed with rags. A cassette is lying on the dashboard, the tracks neatly listed in Emily's writing. I shall pick it up and feed it to the machine.

John has a dream about my father. He tells me it over breakfast, when I am still half asleep.

We have been visiting some farm, and we are making our way back down the hill. My father is with my mother somewhere higher up. Then we hear a commotion in the crowd behind us.

We go back to see what it is, and it is my father. He has collapsed unconscious on the ground. Together we load his body on to some kind of pallet, while my mother watches. We carry him back down the hill, towards the car. And then when we look at him, we see he has changed into a baby. He is asleep, swaddled in blankets.

'What do we feel, when we see he has changed into a baby?' I ask John.

'I don't know.' He tries to remember. 'I think we're all nonplussed. We're just wondering what on earth we're going to do with him when we get home.'

'You never *stuck* at anything, that was your trouble!' my mother would say to me. 'You got tired of Brownies. You got tired of Guides. You got tired of the piano. You only went riding for two years, and then you got sick of it.'

'What do *you* think?' I would try to ask my father, when I dropped out of university.

He would quote his own mother: 'Once you put your hand to the plough . . .'

Now he is fond of reminding me that we live in a culture of broken marriages. He is so happy that John and I and the girls are still together.

'A man boasted to his friend that he was the perfect husband. Whatever his wife asked him to do, he always did immediately, without protest.

' "I have to hear this with my own ears," the second man said.

118

'They went to the first man's house. The second man stood at the gate waiting, while the first man went in to his wife. As he went in, the wind caught at the front door and slammed it behind him.

' "That's right!" his wife called from upstairs. "Tear the door off its hinges!"

'So the first man pulled at the front door with all his strength until it came off in his arms.

'The next night the two men met in the pub. "I bet you five pounds you can't do it again!" the second man said.

'They staggered back to the first man's house. This time he closed the door with exaggerated care. But as he climbed the stairs to his wife, he tripped and fell, reaching out to catch at whatever might break his fall. "That's right!" she shrieked. "Tear all the pictures from the walls and smash them!" So the first man pulled down all the pictures in the house and piled them in the back yard. Then he got a big hammer and smashed them to pieces.

'The next night the two men met in the pub again. They drank until closing-time. Then the second man said, "I bet you fifty pounds you can't do it again!" They staggered back to the first man's house. They were so drunk they could hardly hold each other up.

'The second man waited in the dark by the gate. He heard the door closing quietly. He heard the stairs creak. He heard the first man undressing. Then he heard a tiny chink, as if the first man had accidentally brushed against something as he got into bed.

' "That's right!" he heard the man's wife say drily. "Empty the whole chamber-pot over yourself!" '

Every Sunday at about 4.30 one of us makes a pot of tea. Halfway through his cup my father looks at the clock. 'Is that the time already? I suppose we'd better see about it soon.'

'No hurry,' I say. 'Whenever you're ready.'

We still have all the time in the world. In the time it takes him to get downstairs on John's arm I know I can collect up the tea-things and take them down to the kitchen, unload and re-load the dishwasher, get the laundry in and fold it, put my own shoes and coat on, find my car keys, collect up his scattered belongings and line up his wheelchair in the hall, next to the bottom step. I still have time to watch them come down the last few stairs, my father sideways on, clinging to the banisters with both hands, John half supporting his weight, giving him gentle directions: 'Move your left foot over this way a bit, Eric'; 'Let go now with that hand'; 'Don't sit down yet. Let's get your coat on you first.'

Sometimes, just at the top of the stairs, my father starts to cry. As I fold up the laundry or look for his glasses in their pink plastic case, I stop what I am doing and hear him wailing above my head. I go and wait at the bottom of the stairs for them to come down.

He is clinging to the banisters and wailing. 'It's terrible to be so helpless,' he sobs over and over again.

I go up to where he is and hug him. 'You're not *all that* helpless,' I say. 'There are lots of things you can still do. You're doing all right. Look. We're over halfway there already.'

One day I shall buy a ticket and leave. I shall sit between the window and a man in a dark suit. Soon after we pull out of London he will snap open the briefcase on his dark cloth knees and look at his documents. His hands will come out of dark cloth sleeves. He will be wearing what looks like a wedding ring. His metal ballpoint will wander across the paper, marking things of importance. In the seat opposite another man in another suit of a slightly different shade will shake his newspaper into a convenient shape and begin to do the crossword. Across the gangway two more men, one in a raincoat, will exchange a few remarks before falling asleep. A well-dressed older woman will be quietly reading a book.

I shall try to travel light. The minimum of clothes, my oldest jeans and shirts and pullovers. Socks. Underwear. No books. No ornaments, pictures, personal possessions. No photographs. I shall be wise enough by then to do without all that. I shall be wise enough by then to cover the walls with a wealth of the obscenest graffiti. Or to make the floorboards shake with something louder than singing.

There will be a low table in front of my window. The sun will fall across it obliquely, through one of the angled panes, obliterating the ring-marks with surface reflections. I shall reach out and take the battered metal case in my hand.

The old clasp will resist me. It will have been so long since I last looked inside. Then the lid will spring back and his dark glasses will lie, still shaking, in their oval metal box. The old leather side-pieces are cracked and worn; one of the wire arms is broken, stuck together with masking tape. I shall lift them out gently and lay them in the pool of sunlight. The moving leaves outside will mottle the dark lenses in a pattern of green and gold, like a pond.

I shall wake to another life, swimming to consciousness slowly and feeling the strange sheets twist between my toes. It will be light already, lighter than I remember, closer to the sun. I shall wrap the faded quilt round my shoulders and drag it to the window, the old multicoloured fabric spreading out and trailing behind me over the polished floorboards. In the bay of light that is the window I shall lean and look, suspended over the city, surrounded by leaves.

A sky as pale and deep as water will hold the trees floating. Below and beyond the branches the roofs of the city will reflect the sun, bright patches of red-brown, red, coral. I shall unfasten the sash and push the window up as far as it will go. I shall sit on the sill and lean out as far as I dare. I shall almost be able to touch the branches. And below me I shall hear the rumble of traffic, business, people, the rhythmic comings and goings of trains.

The house I shall choose to live in will be very high, a strange tall Victorian house among trees. And my room will be at the top. I shall look out at leaves. Through and beyond them will be lower, flatter roofs, the muffled noises of the town. A strange, idiosyncratic house full of changing levels. A deep brick footpath between high walls will pass it in front, an unmade gravel road will lead to the other front door on the other side. With the agent's paper still clutched in my hand I shall approach first one façade and then the other, wondering where to knock.

'What do you have?'

'I'm sorry?'

'Have. For breakfast. Tea and toast, eggs, porridge?'

I shall forget that I am not hungry. I shall nod, without speaking. I shall watch her as she lifts a cover on the Aga. I shall feel a gust of warmth. Then she will pour milk and water into a saucepan and put it on to boil.

When it's ready she will bring it to me. She will give me the milk and the golden syrup. I shall have to stop myself from trying to write my name with the spoon.

It will be like being on holiday. I shall come out of the lower front door and stand in the garden, blinking.

The city below me will still be in sunshine. I shall make my way down the path to the uneven steps at the bottom and let myself out through the lower front gate. Then I shall follow the little sunken brick pathway between waist-high walls overhung with shrubs and flowering plants. It could be anywhere, the beginning of the world. The path will twist slightly and go on into the centre, suddenly opening on to a small cobbled square full of shops, then losing itself in a banal, crowded street. I shall start to buy things: dried flowers, a blue glass vase, a strange pottery creature, half man, half fish. It will remind me of my father.

As I am going home, a group of small children will gather behind me, talking and giggling, and I shall have to turn round. There will be four of them, two older girls and two little boys in tow. The oldest of them will be about eleven. At first I shall think they are asking me for food.

But no, it is money they want, and that only for someone else, someone who will have died. One of them will have a cardboard tray suspended round her neck with ribbons, and in it countless little paper flags on pins. 'What's it for?' I shall ask them.

'The famine,' they will say.

'Are you a recognized charity?'

I shall have made her anxious. She will look down and twist the toe of her shoe on the pavement.

I shall repeat my question.

She will look straight at me. 'No. I don't think so. Does it matter?'

'I expect it does. It's probably illegal, what you're doing. You need a licence to sell flags, almost certainly.'

She will move back a little as if to turn away in discouragement. But then she will say, 'We only did it ourselves. Look, we didn't ask anyone for anything. We made them all ourselves.'

I shall look more closely. Until now I shan't really have noticed the flags. They will all be different, hand-drawn, hand-coloured, with wax crayons and coloured pencils and felt-tipped pens. The shapes themselves will be slightly irregular, right angles cut quickly by eye. They will seem to have pictures of ears of corn on them.

'So I see,' I shall say drily.

'They need the money anyway. For the famine. They haven't got anything to eat.'

'Half the people are dead already. It won't make any difference to them.'

'But it'll help the people in their families. The children left behind. And if there's any money left over, it'll do for the next time.'

'There won't be any left over,' I shall say.

She will fidget with the flags in the tray, turning them over so the pictures are uppermost. Then she looks up at me again. 'Will you buy one?'

'How much are they?'

'Five pence each.'

'How many have you got?'

She will think for a moment. Then she will say, 'Ninety-seven.'

I shall feel in my purse and pull out a five-pound note. 'Give me the tray.' She will smile at me suddenly. 'Here, put it round my neck. I'll take them all.'

When I get back to the house, the holiday feeling will have left me. There will be big clouds in the sky now, swimming across to blot out the sun. One of them will be over the garden as I stand there on the path, feeling for my key. It will make the grass look longer and greener. The little statue on the sloping lawn will seem dingier. The tall trees will meet overhead.

I shall climb the first flight of stairs and stop for a moment by the other, upper front door to get my breath. Then I shall go on up again, quietly in case I should meet someone and have to explain. I shall reach my room at the top of the last flight, and sigh. I shall unpack all my things.

The last thing will be the children's flags. There will be so many of them, and they will be so small. With Blu-Tack I shall fix them to the walls in little paper sheaves, above my pillow, on the far wall, to the right of the bay window where the morning sun will strike them. When I close my eyes, I shall still be able to see them, the small ears standing straight and tall, turned greenish by the reflected light of leaves.

Somehow I shall get through the days. The nights will pass. Sometimes I shall sleep almost well. Only occasionally I shall gasp as I remember, as if someone had punched me suddenly, hard enough to do real damage.

I shall wake at three, before the daylight has even started. Total darkness. The street-lamps between the trees will have gone off hours ago. My throat will be as dry as sand.

I shall have been dreaming. The bedclothes will still be wet with my anxiety. I shall be able to feel them clinging to me as I try to turn over. My toes will be tangled in a plait of something long and slippery which will be trying to catch my legs and knot them together so I can never escape. I shall feel it flop to the floor. I shall sit up, sweating, listening to my heart. Perhaps it has receded. Perhaps it will slither away under the door or between the cracks of the floorboards and my heart will be able to stop pounding its distress-signal, and I shall die. But the thing will still crouch in the shadows somewhere, and the irregular, accelerated heartbeat will go on.

One morning when I wake the trees will look almost as if they are alive. It will have rained during the night, and gusts of wet wind will have floated some of the brown leaves to the ground so that the lines of the branches are more visible.

I shall go down to the kitchen. I shall get myself a piece of toast and a mug of coffee. I shall read my way idly through a newspaper that someone will have left on the cloth.

And then I shall see it. Something will catch my eye, so small I shall hardly be able to make out the letters. 'Peacefully, during the night of . . .' And I shall sit back in my chair and see it all, my childhood, his bent shape behind the Zimmer-frame, the things we shall never do now, together or alone. And I shall be free to go back.

Just before my father's birthday he gets a letter from the DVLA, informing him that his driving-licence is about to expire. If he wants to apply for a new one, he must fill in the enclosed form and return it with the old licence and a fee of six pounds. 'I'll have to go over and find my licence,' he says.

'You could fill in the form first,' I tell him.

It takes him about twenty minutes to read the form. Then he says, 'I'll have to go over to Wadhurst to find my old licence.'

'Where do you keep it?'

'In the black box.'

'The black box is at our house. I can go through it for you.' I look across at the form in his lap. I can read the questions. *Do you have any problems with your lower limbs? Have you ever suffered from any of the following?* 'Why don't you see how you get on with the form first?' I ask him.

The next Sunday he brings the DVLA form to our house, along with his library book and newspaper and the three pairs of glasses. 'Have you found my driving-licence?' he asks me.

I tell him I haven't. 'You did say it was in the black box? You do mean the black metal box, the one with the key?'

'No, no. Not that one. The black box.'

'Which black box?'

'The one by my bed.'

'That's a brown wooden box,' I tell him. 'It's full of old *Legal Executives*. You can't mean that one.'

'No, no, not a wooden box!'

'What box, then? What *is* it made of?'

He looks perplexed. 'I don't know. You know the one. Not wood. Not metal. Something a bit plasticky.'

I don't remember any plasticky box. 'I'll go over and have a look for it next week,' I say.

Yesterday I drew back the curtain on my father's landing, the curtain that has been closed for a year. I pulled it back and saw the bright mustard yellow of the lichen on the tiles of the garage roof. There was jasmine in next-door's garden. I saw clouds. Even though the sky was grey, it was amazing how much extra light there was. His carpet went a paler shade of green. The walls were lit up. And I saw that all down the stairs the wall and banisters were covered with his grey fingermarks.

He is like a child now, with his walking. He runs his hands over the walls and furniture the way a child does, as if to check it is all still there, as if to make certain he isn't dreaming. He doesn't trust the Zimmer. Whenever he can, he lets go of it and puts his weight on some piece of furniture. It's the chair-arms he likes, uphol-stered and solid, something to stop him falling off the edge of his life, something he can recognize from way back.

*

126

One day we are going through stuff in my father's attic when Emily calls me over. 'Hey, Mum! Look at this!' She takes it out of the faded blue envelope and opens it into a pale oval. It is about six inches long, streaked with something white and opaque along the creases. It is thinner than paper, more fragile, a giant moon of honesty. We can see our fingers through it. A shred of skin has stuck to the gum on the flap. I detach it and it breaks off, crumbling. I refold the membrane carefully and slip it back in. I turn the envelope over. 'Walter Eric Wicks,' my grandmother has written. '1st August, 1912. Caul.' At first I think the handwriting is my own mother's.

My mother was always frightened that I would get pregnant. 'If you do,' she told me fiercely, 'you can't stay here with us, you know that. You'll have to go away, to a home. And the baby will have to be adopted.'

I never knew whether to laugh or cry.

One night I dream I offer some friends of mine a lift home, and then I can't remember where I parked the car. We wander the streets of Tonbridge. We are pacing the aisles of shiny cars in the car-park. My father stands on tiptoe and scans the horizon for the familiar white metal roof. But nothing here looks like mine. I am getting more and more embarrassed.

Then I begin to feel sick. I lean over and out of my mouth comes a turd, a long coiled albino turd like a white snake. It flops on the ground as if it were made of rubber and rebounds slightly, steaming. My mother looks at it, concerned. 'That's rather nasty,' she says.

One summer Sunday when I go to Greenfield House to collect him, my father seems unusually subdued. He is wearing his tweed and corduroy cap, even though the temperature is in the seventies. Under it he seems to have shrunk. I get him into the car. I load the wheelchair, the Zimmer-frame, his *Mail on Sunday*, his library book, his three pairs of glasses. I drive him to our house. I stop the car outside our front door. 'What's the matter?' I ask him.

'Oh, I don't know . . .'

'There's something the matter, isn't there? Are you all right?'

'Oh, yes. I'm all right.' But he looks miserable.

'Has something happened at Greenfield House?' I ask him.

'Well . . . No. Not really.' He seems to reconsider. 'Well . . . Yes, in a way. I suppose I was a bit mean to Vera.'

'This morning?'

'Yes. No. I don't know. I think it may have been yesterday.'

'What did you do?'

'Oh . . . Nothing much. You know that awful noise she makes. That silly blubbering. It goes on and on. And in the end it gets to you. And I suppose I wasn't very nice.'

'Were you rude to her?'

'Well, not rude exactly. I didn't *say* anything. But you know that noise she makes?' He mimics it sarcastically for my benefit. 'Well, I did it back to her.'

I hesitate. 'She can't help it,' I say gently.

'Well, maybe she can't. But that's no reason to keep making that stupid blubbering noise all the time!'

I shrug. 'Well, it doesn't matter. I don't suppose she even heard you.'

'But the nurses did. A couple of the young ones were there. I think they took rather a dim view of it.'

I lean over and put my arm round him. 'Stop worrying. I'm sure it would get on anyone's nerves in the end. I'll have a word with them about it, if you like.'

A few days later I mention it to Sister Latham. 'Oh, my father was a bit upset the other day . . .' I tell her about Vera. 'He thought perhaps he'd been a bit mean to her.'

Sister Latham looks at me and smiles. 'He *is* a bit mean sometimes,' she says.

I look back at her kind, tired face. I grin back at her.

She laughs. 'Well, he *is* mean . . .'

*

My father is reading a library book, a Francis Durbridge thriller. He is on page eleven.

Every week he brings it with him to our house, and every week it sits on the dresser unopened, a piece of tired paper always marking the same place. John teases him about it gently.

'How's the book going, Eric?'

'Oh. All right. It's a bit slow. Not all that easy to get into.'

Sometimes when I am at Greenfield House, the woman from the library comes round with a bag of new offerings. But my father clings to his one book. She renews it as many times as she can. Then she exchanges it for something else.

And now this second book goes backwards and forwards with my father each week between Greenfield House and our kitchen, the same dog-eared bookmark a couple of pages in.

We are on our way back to Greenfield House. In my rear-view mirror I can see John's face, cut in two by the horizontal bars of the Zimmer-frame. 'One of these Sundays I must drive over to Heathfield to see Peggy,' my father says.

There is a silence, half filled by Villa-Lobos's aria and the sound of the engine. Then I say carefully, 'Daddy, I think you're getting a bit confused. Peggy died.'

At first he doesn't believe me. 'I know *Victor* died. But not Peggy.'

'Yes. She did. She was terribly old and frail. She was ill for a long time. Don't you remember?'

'How long ago was it?'

'About six months ago,' John says.

My father is quiet for a moment. Then he says softly, 'Oh.' And then, 'But I wanted to see her.'

His short-term memory is going. If I have to miss a visit, he often doesn't remember whether he has seen me or not. Now he is forgetting things that happened months ago. The shadow is getting longer, reaching backwards to blot out the landscape further and further from where he is.

129

One of these days he will look at me and say, 'We'll talk to Joy about it when she comes in.' And this time I shall be the one to break the news.

The day before I leave to fly to Virginia I go out and buy my father three pairs of jogging pants. 'They'll be easier for him,' Sister Latham explains to me. 'I've talked it over with Eric, and he agrees.'

I choose the trousers carefully, before collecting my traveller's cheques and buying a few last-minute things I have forgotten. It is hard to decide if he is medium or small. Whichever size I get, the legs will be too long. If my mother were here, she would make tucks in them.

But I find myself grinning as I pay for them and pick up the plastic bag. It is as if he is suddenly some kind of athlete.

When I was growing up, I would nag my mother sometimes to make me dresses. And she would do it. But she hated it. She was always frightened in case she cut them out wrong.

In his room at Greenfield House my father has a photo-cube on top of his television. It is old. The photographs were taken fifteen years ago now, at Emily's christening. Always, when I go up to his room on a Sunday evening to put away his coat and cap, my mother smiles out at me. Emily smiles out from her arms.

Always I go over to her and pick her up and look at them both for a moment. Then I turn the cube round to the picture of my father, the baby's long white shawl trailing, her small face frowning at me.

And always, the next time I see it, the cube is turned to show my mother again, the two of them always caught in that smile.

I dream my parents come in late one evening. I am sitting waiting for them by the fire. I want them to stay and talk to me, but they say they are too tired.

I get out a slab of fruit cake I have made and offer it to them. At first they shake their heads. I cut the cake into slices. It is rich and moist in the centre. In the end they change their minds and sit down with me, their plates balanced on their knees.

And as they eat they begin to revive. The tiredness rolls off them like a skin. They get younger and younger. They will stay with me now until the sun comes up over the roofs of the houses.

I unlock the black metal box and lift the lid. It falls back on to the floor, leaving its bent hinges. A musty smell rises round me, something that clings to my clothes and my hands. I turn over the brittle envelopes full of old papers and glance at their contents. His demob papers, my mother's birth certificate, a list of extras (supplementary power-points, heated towel-rail, retractable loft-ladder) he specified for the Wadhurst house. I empty out one envelope and find a collection of handwritten references on good-quality headed paper: 'Miss Joyce Woolger, has been nurse to my three children for five months and it is with very much sorrow that she is leaving me now, but I sail for India tomorrow, and to my great regret I am unable to take her with me . . . When nurse came to me the baby then aged just two months was so delicate and ill, that I never thought he would grow up, but now he is the picture of health well above the average weight and people stop to look at him as he is such a wonderful picture of health. This is entirely nurses doing and I can not thank her enough for what she has done for him. I would like to add that she has looked after the other children equally well, they have improved in manners wonderfully, and they all adore her.

'Also she is a delightful person to have in a house, and I am more sorry than I can say to have to part with her.'

In the early morning I dream that I am wandering naked in the streets, trying to get help. I need to buy clothes, but I can't go into a shop because I am naked, and there is no one who will do it for me.

Then I find myself in a kind of theatre, the only member of the audience in the pink-upholstered cage of a strange lift. I decide not to be frightened. And while I am in the lift I can already foresee the next scene, when I shall crawl out among toddlers and bright toys. I shall let myself be needy and irresponsible. I shall laugh and cry. Everything I allow myself to do will be foreseen and catered for.

I crawl out of the lift and sit on the floor with the others. I start to play. The playgroup leader notices that I haven't got anything on, and I hear her phoning my mummy. I tell her I want a T-shirt, a big one, a boy's one, and she brings it to me almost at once.

At the end of the day my mother comes to take me. She is pretty and young. I tell her how lovely she is, and she looks puzzled. I ask her questions about my past, and she begins to look worried.

My father comes out of the bathroom in a dressing-gown, coughing. He is big and tall. I hug him tight round his waist and he laughs at me because I am so passionate and fierce and he is so proud of me – his little son. But I am worried about his cough. I can see into the future and I know that it is something serious, something he will soon die of. And I love them both. I can't bear to lose either of them. They are so good and so beautiful. I love them disinterestedly, because they are complete strangers.

My friends sometimes told me how lucky I was. 'Your parents are so lovely!' they would say. 'You can always say anything to them. You can tell them anything you like.'

When I was very small, he would come into my bedroom sometimes late, when he got back from a dance, to kiss me. I can remember his beery smell. '*Reeking* of beer!' my mother would say, laughing, in humorous repetition of my father's own mother. On weekend mornings, while he was still dozing, I would snuggle in with him and try to wake him up.

As far as I remember, neither of my parents ever smoked. They disliked smoking, though they would tolerate it for my aunt's sake, or for their friends'.

One lunch-time my uncle and aunt were eating with us. My aunt had been smoking when she was called away to the phone. The cigarette she had just lit was burning away steadily in the ashtray, the delicate grey cylinder of ash lengthening, eating inwards as we watched.

Then my mother leaned forwards and picked it up. She knocked the ash off. Then she began to puff awkwardly at the filter, laughing at our astonished faces. 'Well,' she said, half apologetically, 'it will be wasted otherwise.'

Every Sunday lunch-time I clear the table and load the plates and cutlery into the dishwasher. I gather up the untouched scraps from my daughters' plates and put them in the refrigerator for the next day, as I always have. I throw my father's away.

He hardly ever mentions my writing, or seems even to remember that I write. But one day he remembers. 'When's your new book coming out?' he asks me.

I hesitate. Then I say, 'April 5th.'

He looks at me blankly. 'April 5th?'

'Yes. Doesn't that date mean anything?'

He shakes his head.

I lean over and give him a kiss on the cheek. April 5th was my mother's birthday.

Sister Latham has recorded the 'New Generation Poets' edition of *The South Bank Show* so that my father can see it. We sit together in front of the lounge television, a group of young nurses hovering behind us. The Greenfield House handyman kneels on the carpet to feed the video into the machine.

'I'm only on for about a minute and a half,' I say. 'Don't get excited.'

But it is an old machine. The video won't work on it. We hear my Pinky and Perky voice rise among the other Pinky and Perky voices, the poems read double-speed at hysteria pitch. 'Something isn't compatible,' I say.

'Oh, what a shame!' Sister Latham is genuinely disappointed. 'And you were so lovely!'

'Don't worry about it.' I laugh. My father is not worrying. But as I drive home I can still see my grey face half transparent on the screen, twitching in its breathless monologue. I see a large grey goldfish turn and swim right through it.

A year after my father has left his house I finally muster the energy to empty his freezer. It is full of remnants of gravy, fat solidified from old joints, blocks of lard, blackberries my mother picked in the lanes nearly three autumns ago. I throw it all out and flick the switch.

Bridget and I take turns at chipping at the ice with a wooden spatula. At first it won't yield. Then suddenly it starts flaking off in huge lumps, falling to the floor of the chest with a clatter. We attack it with our spatula, laughing as the great blocks of ice give way. Then we lean into the freezer to pick it out. Our hands are red with cold. We collect it in plastic bowls. We empty the bowls on to the lawn. As we reverse out of the drive, the grass is still strewn with white splinters like splinters from a block of salt.

Even now my father is almost unreasonably proud of his loft. When I take the estate agent over his house I feel I owe it to my father to show it to him. I get the long stick with the hook on the end that reminds me of a shepherd's crook, and pull down the loft-ladder. A shower of dead flies falls on our heads. Some of them aren't even dead, but still twitching. But I turn on the attic light and the estate agent climbs the aluminium ladder dutifully. 'Look,' I tell him. 'It's all beautifully boarded over. My father's pride and joy.'

My mother was terrified of attics, and caves. She would only go up into the loft very occasionally, when my father forced her to. He would have to stand behind her on the next rung.

And I think of her dead, in some mythical high place, or screaming somewhere under the ground. If she has gone to heaven he will have to get up there with her, get down on his hands and knees with a hammer and a mouthful of nails to board it over, before she can put a foot on the plaster and fall through.

The black metal box is full of old things. My school reports, my father's medals, the gold half-hunter watch one of his clients bequeathed to him. The bottom is littered with books of dead cheque-stubs. My grandmother's death certificate (arteriosclerosis and gangrene, age eighty-three). My own birth certificate. My parents' joint passport, with their two photos. And their marriage certificate, its green waves crossed and recrossed by Reverend Lewis's grey handwriting, complete with errors. 20th January 1942. Her father's profession: Garage proprietor. His father's profession: Chauffeur.

Towards the end of July I drive Bridget out into the country to camp in a friend's garden. It is hot. We open both windows wide, and the green air floods in. We drive along a fast smooth road between young plantations. The road becomes narrower and more overgrown. Then I turn into a lane between converted barns and oast-houses, gardens full of roses. I open the boot and pull out backpack, sleeping-bag, chocolate biscuits, marshmallows to be toasted on sticks over the camp-fire. 'What's this?' I ask her.

She stares at me.

I pull it out from one corner, from behind the tool-box. It is warm and squishy in my hand, a slab of Sainsbury's Ardennes pâté (reduced), still in its packaging, the liquid fat running and bubbling at the edges. I look at the date: *Sell by July 7*. 'Would you like some of this with your marshmallows?'

My daughter wrinkles her nose. She picks up the backpack and sleeping-bag. I lean into the car to smooth out the crumpled seat-cover, tucking it in securely down by the seat-belt anchorage, stroking the warm fleece flat with the palm of my hand.

On the last letter he sent to his sister his writing was so small it was illegible. I put his envelope inside a larger envelope of my own and wrote the address again myself. Otherwise the birthday card with its picture of little girls on a beach would never have reached her.

The wide mouth will smile down at me; the glittering tail will be like nothing I have ever dreamed of. And when he hands me the stick, he will let go too soon.

I can see it, the figure-of-eight string jumping and snagging in the grass as it skitters away from us towards the cliff-edge, the last sea-pinks blowing against nothing.

He will shout something, his words torn away from me by the wind. 'What a *chump*!' he will say.

But then he will put his arm round my shoulders and we'll stand side by side to watch it, the wobbly smile, the glint of the tail as it meets the sea. 'Not your fault,' he will say as I blink back the tears. 'It was me. I let go too soon.'

Then, as he starts the engine and I bite down into my bun, he will turn his head to look at me and wink. 'How about *gold* paper for the next one?'

I shall nod. 'Can I help make it?' I'll ask him with my mouth full.

Once at a party I stumbled into a bright kitchen full of bottles and animated men. They were talking about cars. 'Hey, Sue!' They pounced on me. 'If you could buy any car you liked, what would you choose?'

I looked up from the drink I was pouring. 'I don't know. I've never thought about it. A Fiat 500?'

They stared at me in disbelief. Then the whole room burst out laughing.

In the United States people still put pennies on the railway lines, where they can't be seen, under bridges. The trains run right over them and leave them beaten to new ovals like brass leaves, the faces and lettering on them flattened to nothing.

*

My parents were always completely honest. I can't think of a single lie they ever told me.

The day my mother dies the honeysuckle on the fence is bristling with massed trumpets. The glare of the sun on the pages of my book is almost unsustainable. I only have to hear my father's voice on the telephone to know I have always dreamed exactly this.